p. 41
59
68

Death and Immortality

Death and Immortality

JOSEF PIEPER

HERDER AND HERDER

1969
HERDER AND HERDER
232 Madison Avenue, New York 10016

Original edition: *Tod und Unsterblichkeit,*
Munich, Kösel Verlag, 1968
Translated by Richard and Clara Winston

Contents

I. An Especially Philosophical Subject   10

> Death: a philosophical subject in a special sense.
> The "hub of the wheel": all statements move close
> together. The predefined question situation. There
> is no direct experience of death. Everything is
> uncertain except death. The absolute crisis. "Con-
> stant reassurance about death" (Heidegger). The
> opportunity of love.

II. The Vocabulary of Death   23

> Variety of vocabulary. The problematical aspect
> of euphemism. End of life, loss and lack of refer-
> ence, time and eternity, death personified, dying as
> an act. What is "the living language"? The im-
> permissible simplification.

III. What does "Separation of Body and Soul" mean?   32

> "Separation of body and soul." How is the preced-
> ing connection conceived? Platonism's answer:
> the lute player, the sailor in the boat, the prisoner
> in the cell. The minimizing of dying. Not the body
> dies, but the man. *Anima forma corporis*. The soul
> joined with the body is more similar to God
> (Thomas Aquinas). Death as destruction of the real
> man. The theological protest against idealistic
> minimizing.

IV. A Natural Event or a Punishment?   47

Death something natural? Excludable answers. "The most extreme of all human suffering." The concept of "just punishment." Anaximander's saying. To be punished is no evil. All wickedness either punishment or guilt? Insofar as death is punishment, it is not natural. Is man's state "improper"? The world as *creature*. Death is "in a certain sense according to nature, in a certain sense contrary to nature" (Thomas Aquinas). The inclusion of believed truth. The propriety of experience: sin is something deathly. Death as an aspect of sin. The *necessitas moriendi* and the "deathless" death (Karl Rahner) of paradisiacal man. Christ died not because he had to but because he wanted to. The attitude towards death: forms of non-acceptance. "Freedom towards death"? The lucidity of the interpretation of death as a divinely imposed penalty. What is the meaning of: to accept punishment? Perfect dying.

V. The *Status Viatoris*   83

What happens in death is not merely the end; man also "makes an end." Termination of the *status viatoris*. Existence as "not-yet-being." The last decision. The interplay of necessity and freedom. There is no untimely death. Ending is not necessarily completion.

VI. Death and Freedom   92

Objections to the freedom of ultimate decision. "Death provokes freedom." The "conscious dying" of the condemned. Sartre against Heidegger. Implications of the conception of judgment after death. Mind's superiority over time. The "consciousness" of the dying. The last step on the road

cannot be anticipated. What is the meaning of
"learning to die"?

VII. Immortality—of what?   104

The element of "futurity" in the concept of terminating the *status viatoris*. The disputation on
"immortality of the soul." The "central dogma of
the Enlightenment." Christoph August Tiedge
and Immanuel Kant. Discrediting of the idea of
immortality. Moses Mendelssohn's misinterpreta-
tion of Plato. Plato is no Platonist. What is always
suggested by the indestructibility of the soul: immortality of the entire man.

VIII. Indestructibility and Eternal Life   117

What is the meaning of "imperishability"? "All
the works of God persist for eternity." "Incapable
of not being." By virtue of creation means: by
nature. Creating as real communication of being.
Possible arguments for the indestructibility of the
soul. The meaninglessness of opinion polling. The
soul is indestructible because it is capable of truth.
The mode of being of the "departed soul" is inconceivable to us. If the soul were not by nature
indestructible, no one could receive the gift of
Eternal Life. No "learned question."

Notes   131

It is absurd that we are born; it is absurd that we die.

—Jean-Paul Sartre

*

All I regret is having been born, dying is such a long tiresome business I always found.

—Samuel Beckett

*

Every day is a good day to be born; every day is a good day to die.

—Pope John XXIII

I

An Especially Philosophical Subject

THERE is absolutely nothing between heaven and earth that cannot set us to philosophizing, that is to say to considering the whole of the universe and the whole of existence. This is as true for a tiny grain of matter as for a casual gesture of the human hand. We need not hunt for some object of philosophy which is distinguished by special "sublimity", let alone abstractness. This sort of object is always present; it lies squarely before everyone's eyes.

Nevertheless, there are subjects which must be called "philosophical" in a stronger sense—because it is in their very nature to compel us to consider the whole of existence. Among these specifically philosphical subjects that of "death" holds an incomparable place.

What actually happens, viewed fundamentally and in terms of the whole, when a human being dies? Anyone who asks that question is, of course, not solely concerned with a particular event which took place on such and such a day. One who has been struck by the experience of death is forced to direct his gaze towards the Whole of reality. He thinks of "God and the world", above all of what in the final analysis man is all about. Not that he feels any acute and urgent need to find a *definition* of man, or a description of human nature. In fact, when we are touched by the closeness of death such questions strike us as not very serious, as altogether too minor. What becomes urgent is the riddle of human existence, the "question of our condition". Faced with that, "we can become perplexed even if we can neatly define man and distinguish him from the animals and the angels".[1]

This idea has been expressed all through the ages and in many different ways. In the *Confessions* St Augustine recalls the unexpected death of a friend which had affected and distracted him at the age of nineteen, when he himself was first stepping into adult life. He closes his account with the sentence: *Factus eram ipse mihi magna quaestio*: "I had become a great question to myself."[2] It has been said that this sentence represents "the birth of existential philosophy" from the experience of death.[3]

Thus death has been from time immemorial not only a unique subject for philosophical meditation. Rather, the act of philosophizing itself seems to have first derived its full earnestness from this subject, if indeed it did not receive its first impetus from it—so that death can literally be called "the real inspiring genius of philosophy", without which man "would hardly ever have philosophized".[4] It is not far from this idea to the much more radical proposition which is to be found in Cicero's *Tusculan Disputations*, that philosophizing is nothing else but consideration of death, *commentatio mortis*.[5] Once formulated, this idea has fastened itself like a fishhook in Occidental thinking—not when his thought revolves upon death, but when it revolves upon the essence of philosophy or, to be more precise, when it revolves upon the meaning of philosophizing. Hence, when in twelfth-century Toledo the learned Spaniard Gonzales, one of the great mediators and translators in the history of European thought, collected the traditional definitions of philosophy,[6] he mentioned among them the following: *cura et studium et* _sollicitudo mortis_, that is, philosophizing is not just meditative consideration of death, but nothing less than learning to die. Incidentally, six hundred years earlier Cassiodorus, the friend of Boethius, had noted that such a definition of philosophy was the one most appropriate for a Christian[7]—although it originally sprang, as we know, from the soil of Platonism and the Stoa. Seneca praises the ancient philosophers for teaching how to die;[8] and the _Discourses_ of Epictetus states: "Let others study cases at law, let others practise recitations and syllogisms. You learn to die."[9]

At this point I make a pause. To be sure, I am convinced that such talk of learning to die is an accurate and profound description (and not only of philosophy, incidentally, for it also says something about dying as well—for example, that possibly there can be an "unlearned", a wrong kind of dying; which furthermore suggests that by "dying" is not meant just the purely physiological ending of life, but an act to be performed by man). I know, furthermore, that the phrase was never meant to imply that man should keep his mind exclusively on his "last hour", on parting and departing. (Rather, Michel de Montaigne is quite right when he says: "He who would teach men to die would teach them to live."[10]) True though all that is, in the following pages I do not intend to speak about death in such tones, not in the style of the _adhortatio_ and of movingly summoning up the presence of death. Rather, I shall attempt to illuminate the subject, to explain and clarify, and first of all to examine the question of what really takes place, seen in terms of the Whole, when a man dies. Moreover, I hope to conduct this investigation with the greatest possible objectivity and dispassionateness, and with the utmost impartiality I can muster.

By "impartiality" I mean above all the resolute determination to consider everything, or at any rate not to thrust aside any of the information about death that is available to us, whether this information is offered by physiology and pathology, by the experiences of doctors, priests and prison chaplains, or by the legitimate "sacred tradition".

This inclusion of the believed truth, and the attempt to include it in a meaningful relationship to what we know critically, is an undertaking by nature as problematical as it is indispensable. It always leads—and we cannot expect it to be otherwise—to an enormous complicating of our thinking. It is always more difficult for the believer to philosophize than for one who does not bind himself to the canon of a suprahuman truth. But this time, in consideration of our subject, "death", we must prepare ourselves for such acute tensions in our intellectual structure that we may well be brought close to the border of contradiction.

When we speak of death we find ourselves right at the hub of the wheel. Our problem is not only that the discussion brings to light the consequences hidden in our ordinary opinions, both true and false, about people and life. Our problem is also that the true statements, which can bear the most assorted aspects, move so close together that they seem to get in each other's way, so that the slightest shift in accent can in fact destroy the truth of the whole.

The difficulty begins, incidentally, in finding agreement on what is meant by linking the two concepts of "death" and "immortality". The innocent hearer or reader will usually understand the combination to mean that "death" is the question and "immortality" the answer. He will naturally connect the latter word exclusively with "immortal *soul*".

Yet both these assumptions are highly suspect, if not down-right wrong. We shall revert to this matter later. Neverthe-less, it will be well to keep in mind from the beginning that Plato—amazingly, he of all writers—called immortality a "terrible danger".[11] And St Augustine in his *Soliloquia* asks himself the question: "When you have learned that you are immortal—will that be enough for you?" To which he himself gives the remarkable answer: "It will be something great; but it is too little for me."[12]

There is one thing more we shall have to be clear about: that man, when he attains to critical consciousness, when he begins to consider his ideas on death, by no means begins altogether anew, in neutral indifference, his soul still "an unwritten page", setting foot on an island never yet trod by him. He has already come under the atmospheric influence of those ideas about death which are abroad in his own time. Hence he always approaches his great subject with certain expectations and fears, with his attention riveted to certain aspects of it. For example, for the man of late antiquity, the individual who felt cast back upon himself, isolated and ex-posed by the decay of the great political structures, who sought refuge in the mystery cults, in philosophical sects, and in the rigid self-sufficiency of the Stoa—for this man the very casting of the question was different from what it would be for the man of the late Middle Ages with its *danses macabres* and epidemic outbreaks of panicky fear of death. And, of course, our own thinking as well, before we engage in critical reflection, is in many ways coloured by the influ-ence of current attitudes towards death and dying, by the materialistic disparagement of death no less than by nihilistic defiance of it, as well as by the crass optimism of simply ignoring it—as if the dying of human beings were some sort of "painful episode" that occasionally "still" happens, something it is best not to talk about, at least not in public.[13] Thus we are always, whether we know it or not, "engaged" in one way or another when we ask the question: What is it that happens, fundamentally, when a man dies?

Nevertheless these semiconscious attitudes are not the only operative ones; there are philosophical currents which profoundly characterize any given period and its inhabitants, and from which no one can simply withdraw into some presumably "timeless" epistemological position. Hans Urs von Balthasar[14] has distinguished three great periods in philosophical thinking about death. He calls them the mythic-magical period, the theoretical period, and the existential period. "We stand in the third and cannot return to the first two." The "principle" of this succession, it seems to me, is as patent as it is disturbing: with each succeeding epoch the enigma of death presents itself even more inexorably to the mind. Along with this, it may be expected that those statements about death offered by the traditional creed of Christendom, tested or even thrown into question by the assumptions which are modern at any given time, can suddenly acquire new and unexpected emphases. And this, too, is a process inevitably replete with conflicts. But the sacred tradition simply remains mute if it is not pitted against the present era in such a manner that its perennial message is not only constantly repeated, but newly stated, and thus becomes a real contribution to mankind's never-ending discourse.

What, then, takes place when human beings die? In German, incidentally, the word *sterben*, to die (etymologically related to the English *starve*), is applied exclusively to people —here we have another preconception, apparently decided

14

in advance and fixed. Other words are used for the dying of animals, and the pure spirit perisheth not. Here once again we see what little help it is to consult etymology. Etymologically, the word *sterben* is associated with the idea of becoming stiff. But this immobility of the lifeless body, this element common to both animals and men, which can even be observed more readily in the cadaver of a dead animal, is certainly *not* the characteristic thing, is not what men mean when they speak of dying. What, then, is the characteristic thing?

If after all these preliminary remarks we attempt to take the first step towards answering this question, we find ourselves brought up short once again. Presumably the first step should be to describe, with the greatest possible precision and completeness, the facts provided by direct experience. But who has direct experience of what happens in the process of dying? On what may we lean? It has been said, to be sure, that the physician has an unusually "intimate intercourse with death".[15] This means that his profession compels him to witness the process of dying many times, or else that as a medical scientist he possesses, on the basis of observation and exact measurements of breathing, cardiac activity, condition of the blood (and so on), scientific knowledge of what happens in physiological terms when a person dies. Such knowledge is certainly no small thing; and it is surely indispensable to a full comprehension of death, insofar as anything of the sort can exist. On the other hand, if we ask after the meaning of death not as scientists but "as human beings", it is not the physiological events we are interested in. These are important to medical research and, to be sure, to the individual insofar as physiology holds out the prospect of postponing the moment of death for a while. But even if the process of dying should, happily, be delayed, there is ultimately no stopping it; and he who inquires into the nature of death is solely interested in what truly takes place. Obviously this "what truly takes place" is *not* the cessation of breathing and the heartbeat.

But nobody can have any direct experience of the "real nature" of death—except, possibly, the dying person himself. And it is inherent in the nature of this experience that it is not communicable. One of the permanent insights of modern existential philosophy has been the recognition of this: "Death is not an event"; "by its very essence, death is in every case mine"; "the dying of others is not something which we experience in a genuine sense; at most we are simply 'there alongside' ". Thus Martin Heidegger in *Being and Time*.[16] And Karl Jaspers wrote a few years earlier: "Death is something inconceivable, in fact really unthinkable. What we conceive and think about it are only negations and only subsidiary aspects. . . . Thus in the real sense we do not even experience the death of our neighbour."[17] As Hans Urs von Balthasar has said, we "can no longer turn back" from this existential view.

Nevertheless, a good deal of information highly pertinent to our knowledge of death can be read from the mere fact that men die, which everyone experiences. Quantitative data, however, do not particularly matter. Thus, I do not need to know that year after year approximately forty million people die.[18] Everyone's experience that within his own circle people are constantly dying entirely suffices. This experience is sufficient to justify the conclusion that every man must and will die, including the one who has just arrived at this conclusion.

Here above all, however, it is essential to distinguish between mere abstract, conceptual knowledge and existential knowledge, or as John Henry Newman[19] calls it, between "notional knowledge" and "real knowledge". And we can very well ask whether the existential certainty that we must die would not come to us even if we did not observe dying all around us. There is in fact much reason to think that this certainty of our own death is completely independent of all external experience. Max Scheler[20] has expressed this view with great force: "A man would know in some way that death will overtake him even if he were the sole living being on earth." Now such knowledge—that death awaits every man, whether the knowledge is based on some inner sense of the attributes of his own life or upon experience with the fact of death in the outer world—such knowledge of man's fate as sparing absolutely no one, seems to me a great deal. St Augustine actually regarded this knowledge as one of the key aspects of death; and he evidently considered it requisite to convey this knowledge to his readers, and above all to his hearers, as "real" existential cognition: *Incerta omnia, sola mors certa*:[21] of all things in the world only death is not uncertain. "Everything else about us, good as well as evil, is uncertain. . . . When the child is conceived, perhaps it will be born, perhaps there will be a miscarriage. . . . Perhaps the child will grow up, perhaps not; perhaps it will grow old, perhaps not; perhaps it will be rich, perhaps poor; perhaps honoured, perhaps humiliated; perhaps it will have sons, perhaps not. . . . And the same for whatever other good things you may name. Consider all evils there may be; for all, everywhere, it is true that perhaps they may be, perhaps not. But can you also say of someone: Perhaps he will die, perhaps not? As soon as a man is born, it must at once and necessarily be said: He cannot escape death."[22]

To repeat: if in answering the question of what happens in

the process of human dying we should reply, with full grasp of its import: something happens that everyone expects—we shall have taken a considerable stride, especially when we also bear in mind both the certainty of death and the general experience that the specific time of death is so utterly uncertain. Whenever there has been some serious philosophizing on the theme of *commentatio mortis* this association of certainty and uncertainty has been regarded as virtually its most important motif. "Someone, looking through my tablets the other day, found a memorandum about something I wanted done after my death. I told him what was true, that although only a league away from my house, and hale and hearty, I had hastened to write it there, since I could not be certain of reaching home." So we may read in the *Essays*[23] of Michel de Montaigne, in the chapter headed: "That to philosophize is to learn to die."

Nevertheless, this is not all that can be said on the basis of our experience with men's mortality. We know not only that death awaits every man with certainty at an absolutely unknown moment, but also that in dying something uniquely *ultimate* takes place, a definite departure from "this" life, something irrevocable in the most absolute sense. To be sure, there are other acts and experiences of ours which are in a certain sense ultimate; at any rate we cannot undo them. Once done they are "in the world", and they continue to have their effects, for good and bad. But nothing is so ultimate as death. When a man dies, he crosses a frontier which henceforth remains unalterably behind him; there is no returning. The familiar distinction between "here" and the "beyond" refers explicitly to death and to it alone. Incidentally, this is not a specifically Christian idea (from a Christian point of view, in fact, it would probably have to be stated in more relative and less absolute language). When Plato[24] speaks of *ekei*, "over there", he means the place of the dead. Death is the absolute borderline; what lies on the other side of death is, without the need or the possibility of any more specific definition, simply the "beyond". But because death possesses this finality, it is also serious to the uttermost degree. There is no other way of expressing more extremely that something is utterly serious than by saying: it is a matter of life and death. Death is the absolute crisis.

Although all these empirical findings (inevitability of death, uncertainty of the hour, finality of the parting) have given us a number of insights, our initial question still remains entirely open: the question of what this event really is. What in the final analysis happens when a man dies? This question is still without an answer.

Since there is no direct human experience of death, to which we might look for an answer—must we give up? Must we depend upon suprahuman information? But even that would be closed off if there were not something within ourselves capable of a corroborative response to it, if we were not able to give some kind of acquiescence to it based upon our very own experience.

This is the point to speak of a minute chance which may repose in our witnessing the deaths of other men, in the fact of being "there alongside", a chance that we may after all be able to have some direct experience of death. To be sure, this chance is not present in every case and does not occur "of its own accord", so to speak; but that is implied in the concept of a chance. For if what we can know of death comes to us through the death of others, we are naturally tempted to spare ourselves any real encounter with death, thus fending off the experience of our own death. That has been said many times. "Death is an affair of the others"—that is how it is put in Thomas Mann's *The Magic Mountain*. But the same idea was expressed two hundred years earlier in Edward Young's *Night Thoughts*: "All men think all men mortal but themselves."[25] In Tolstoy's great story, *The Death of Ivan Ilyich*, the mortally ill man suddenly thinks of the textbook specimen of logic. Caius is a man, all men are mortal, therefore Caius is mortal. "The example had seemed to him correct only in relation to Caius. Caius is in fact mortal, and it is all very well for him to die; but for me . . . the matter is entirely different." Martin Heidegger, finally, has generalized this same fact and included it in his magnificent "analysis of ordinary life". Constant reassurance about death is one of the fundamental processes of ordinary life, he says. "The expression (one dies) sows the impression that death is always operative in the third person—not we, not you, but they are those who die."[26]

But we have said that alongside this widespread temptation to avoid meeting the reality of death there is an opportunity for a direct experience of one's own death in witnessing the death of others. But this is granted to us only on a single premise. The premise is *love*. This statement, however, must instantly be shielded and defended against a whole swarm of misunderstandings which, we are aware, arise as soon as the words are said.

In the shock that is inflicted upon us by the death of a beloved person there is something that is neither pity nor grief at the loss. "To love a being is to say, 'Thou, thou shalt not die!'"—this memorable sentence by Gabriel Marcel[27] penetrates, it seems to me, far more deeply into the heart of the matter. And what is imparted to the lover faced with the actual death of the beloved person who "must not" die is that he himself experiences this death—for in this case, it is not really "another" who is dying—not just from outside, but as ✓ if from within. He is accorded an experience which comes as close as humanly possible to the dying person's experience of his own death.

The word "lover" should not be misunderstood in romantic terms, as if we were speaking of *amour-passion*, of passionate love as the prerequisite for this kind of experience. (On the contrary, passion may be the form of love that does *not* fit this case.) Rather, we are speaking of that wholly selfless affirmation which can be read in the eyes as they gaze upon the beloved, an affirmation which says: How good that you *are*! In philosophical literature I have encountered only one writer who has expressed this matter with complete clarity: Paul Ludwig Landsberg. In his brief, almost forgotten book, *Die Erfahrung des Todes*, he says: "A single act of personal love suffices to . . . make us able to feel the essential core of human death."[28] *Ubi amor, ibi oculus*:[29] these ancient words assert that love gives one the means for seeing and experiencing. In relation to death, these words suddenly acquire a truly illuminating significance. He who does not flinch from the full impact of the death of a beloved person but identifies with that death by virtue of his love, can have some sense of the nature of death—even if only to the extent that the information available in the great tradition loses a little of its strangeness for him, becomes not only comprehensible, but also is acceded to, or at least somewhat responded to, by a new knowledge within himself.

The refusal of empathy and the impossibility of experiencing one's own death are obviously two sides of the same coin. To hold aloof from death is to cheat oneself of the profoundest insight into one's own personal reality. To be sure, there is also the other aspect of the matter: No one experiences the pain and dreadfulness of death and dying so thoroughly as one who loves.

II

The Vocabulary of Death

IF, as is only proper, we begin by considering the vocabulary, the names and various coinages with which the living language denotes, paraphrases or suggests death and dying, we come upon an odd complication. In this case, however, it does not take us utterly by surprise. At first sight, of course, we find an almost overwhelming multiplicity of terms which seem to reflect the infinite variety of aspects that the matter itself presents. But beyond that, quite a few of the words seem intended *not* to name the reality of the thing, rather to ✓ obscure it, make it unrecognizable and divert our attention to something else. This remarkable phenomenon of euphemism, of extenuating language which avoids calling a spade a spade, is in itself an extremely difficult matter to fathom. For Jews of the Old Testament, it was forbidden to pronounce the name of God. Many peoples have felt that calling a threatened disaster by its proper name would somehow summon it forth. Thus euphemistic circumlocutions are born. The goddesses of vengeance are called the Well-disposed ones; the devil comes to be called Old Nick, actually the name of St Nicholas to whom one appealed for protection against him; the drink which kills is given the innocent name of "poison", from the Latin *potio*, a drink, potion. Thus a great many elements enter into the manufacture of such euphemistic language—motives ranging from religious awe and superstitious fear to more or less conscious deceptions and self-deceptions.

Let us begin by a survey of the vocabulary. We discover first of all the scarcely surprising fact that many of the words used in our languages to signify the death and dying of human beings focus on the simple fact of the end of physical life. We say: He has expired; he is no more; it's over; he has passed away. Other terms speak more precisely and vividly of the immediately observable physiological fact of becoming inanimate, "falling asleep", "dropping off", "never waking up" (from anaesthesia, say, during surgery). In ordinary usage none of these words is meant to cover very much more than the simple fact. Of course someone may say, with the intention of making a real statement and in a markedly "significant" tone which deliberately goes far beyond ordinary usage: It's all over; he is no more; his life is ended. But such a statement, while it has a certain force, nevertheless—if it is not flatly wrong—calls for some supplementing, if not correcting, certainly further specification. Of course the physiologist is right when he defines death as "the extinction of the individual system",[1] or as "the irreversible cessation of the vital processes, especially of metabolism",[2] or as the "irrevocable loss of life".[3] "That is dead which can never again be viable."[4] Nevertheless, such sentences, when examined closely, prove to be remarkably meaningless (they have with some justice been bluntly called "insipidly tautological"[5]). Moreover, they lose all validity as soon as they are taken as absolutes, as final and conclusive descriptions of human death, without amendment by the truth of other, no less valid testimony.

The phrase, incidentally, which calls death a sleep and dying a falling asleep, although originally a biblical[6] figure, may be seen as an attempt to conceal the gravity of death and thus to falsify its reality. Sören Kierkegaard[7] was forever taking issue with this very notion that death is "night" and "gentle sleep"; that is a sentimental picture, not a true one, he says. Shakespeare, it would seem, has something similar in mind when he makes Hamlet, dagger drawn against himself, wish for death as for a sleep ("To die, to sleep; to sleep") but suddenly start back at the thought: "For in that sleep of death what dreams may come . . . must give us pause."

A good many of our words for death and dying express what happens in the community when one of its members dies. We say: the dead man has left us; he has gone from us for ever; he has departed; the husband has "lost" his wife, the mother her child. Once again these phrases convey little more than the simple fact—which, to be sure, so deeply affects the individual—that the daily intercourse of living and conversing together has been cut off. And it is again true that the same words instantly call for more precise definition and perhaps correction if they are used in a larger, let alone ultimate sense. At least the question must be asked: Does death really mean absolute "loss" and total absence of further connection? In what sense does the "departed" leave the world of men and enter into a "hereafter" in which he is absolutely inaccessible to the living, or at any rate unaddressable?

There is another class of words which deal with the relationship between death and time. One who dies ends his days; he passes out of time; he is called to eternity. In a phrase such as the last, of course, the border is crossed which separates mere denotation from interpretation. But even the mere statement that dying means leaving the realm of temporal existence—even this is difficult enough to grasp. The exact meaning eludes us; we shall come back to this matter. What concerns us at the moment is only to list, or rather to hear, as impartially as possible the multifarious statements on death which are actually contained in language as it is spoken and "understood" by ourselves day after day. These very phrases about time and eternity, though of course nourished by the "sacred tradition", have passed into normal, unconsidered speech;[8] the deceased has "gone to his eternal rest", or to his "eternal home".

Since we have agreed to discuss our subject with utter sobriety and with the sole aim of achieving maximum clarity, I must say something about the danger of taking such a phrase as death's being a passing to eternal rest in a false, euphemistic sense. There are two ways of understanding the phrase: one can understand it to mean that dying of itself, and hence always *eo ipso*, amounts to entering into eternal rest, or one can understand it as expressing a *hope*, the—to be sure well-founded—hope that the dead person may have come to his eternal rest as his true destination. I believe that only the second interpretation is possible for the Christian. How otherwise could he seriously say in prayer: *Requiem aeternam dona eis, Domine*! On the other hand, it seems to me that the secular talk about resting under the sod ("May the earth lie lightly upon you"[9]—and so on) is at best pseudo-poetic, ineffectual phrasemaking, if not simply empty babble and self-deception—surely we need not go any further into that.

In death notices we may occasionally read: He has returned his soul to God. This, too, is a formula drawn originally from the vocabulary of the Christian Church that has become part of the thinking and the speech of European man. However, the concept of dying implicit in these words is not easily set forth in a few sentences. "Soul" here does not simply mean what it does in the other common phrase "body and soul"; *anima* is rather the noun for the physical life, taken as a whole. But the important thing about such a phrase is its implication that the dying person is not only a sufferer, but also a doer. It is not just that in dying something happens to us; rather, dying is simultaneously an act by the person himself, and moreover an act in which he has command over his *anima*, that is, over his life, over himself, in a way that is denied to him up to the moment of death.

This idea, it seems, is quite incompatible with the other conception of "Death the Reaper", the Grim Reaper with his scythe, the hunter who pursues us and ultimately "catches up" with us, brings us to bay and hurls us to the ground. And yet such images are also part and parcel of men's linguistic habits. Death as a murderous enemy, a merciless marauder who comes entirely from outside, breaking into our dwelling and overpowering us—such conceptions are widespread; they do not exist merely in the context of late medieval Dances of Death. The New Testament[10] too calls death the "last enemy" and exclaims triumphantly, almost scornfully: "Where is your victory." In classical tragedy, the *Alcestis* of Euripides,[11] death appears as one of the *dramatis personae*, death "hostile to men and hateful to the gods"; Apollo enters into a dispute with him, and comments ironically: "Death is growing witty; that is new."

Of course no one will deny that this metaphor is an apt one for certain aspects of death. But we are also clearly aware that such figures have their flaws. Obviously it becomes simply false if it is taken to mean that man "of his own accord" would not die, if death did not descend upon him from the outside, performing an act of violence like a murder —that is, that death is not so much a matter of dying as of being killed. And yet there is, as we have said, some truth in this notion, for which many other words and images could be cited, such as the blowing out of the lamp of life, or the idea of the Fates cutting the thread. Yet along with this, the alternative concept should not be obscured or concealed: that we ourselves, in living our life away, are on the way to death; that death ripens like a fruit within us; that we begin to die as soon as we are born; that this mortal life moves towards its end from within, and that death is the forgone conclusion of our existence here.

Georg Simmel, in his book on Rembrandt[12] published in 1917, made the acute and instantly persuasive remark that Rembrandt's great portraits represent people who already carry death within themselves as a *character indelebilis* of life. It is written on their faces that they will die, he says, whereas a good many of the portraits of Italian Renaissance painting suggest the deceptive idea that these people can be laid low only by violence, by the stroke of a dagger, say, or by poison. I would say that each of these two aspects contains one part of reality; but each also needs to be balanced by the other; neither one is right in itself. On the one hand "natural" death, death purely from old age, is a rare occurrence (once in a hundred thousand cases, say the statisticians). But on the other hand, even in violent, "non-natural" death, whose cause may be an accident, an infection, a proliferation of cells, or a crime—even then the death takes place simultaneously from within, as the result of life, as the last step of a way initiated at birth, as an act of the dying person himself. Evidently the fatal wound from which the lifeblood ebbs is not identical with dying. And even in suicide two entirely different things take place. One is firing the bullet into the temple, the drinking of poison, the leap from the bridge; the other is dying itself. And in that dying there is not only a blow from outside, but at the same time an action, an act proceeding from the personal centre and terminating life from within, an act by which the life attains to the result intended from the start.

In recognizing this we sweep aside a deception which men have long employed, particularly in classical antiquity, in the attempt to overcome the fear of death. I refer to the sophism of not encountering death, which Epicurus seems to have been the first to formulate; "Death is nothing to us; for as long as we are, death is not here; and when death is here, we no longer are. Therefore it is nothing to the living or the dead."[13] The same argument, or variations of it, has been repeated many times since, from Lucretius and Cicero to Montaigne and Ernst Bloch; but the idea has not thereby become more credible. As soon as we give some serious consideration to the knowledge embodied in the very language of men, we realize that we cannot take comfort in this evasion.

However: what do we mean by "the language of men"? What belongs to the realm of the "living language", which we have tried to probe for whatever it can tell us? And what lies outside that realm; where does the boundary run? Do not the things that philosophers, scientists and poets have said about death also belong to the vocabulary of the living language? This question, of course, reaches far beyond our theme, and I shall not give a formal answer to it now. I shall not even attempt one; I capitulate in the face of its difficulty. Nevertheless, a few examples will make my distinction clearer.

The following phrases of Goethe occur in a letter written to Zelter a few years before his death: "Let us continue our efforts until . . . summoned by the World Spirit, we return

into the ether."[14] I am not contending that such phraseology
has no place in our investigation—although in the case of
Goethe we must always take account of his amazing skill at
ironically disguising and masking himself ("My seeming
liberalistic detachment . . . is only a mask . . . behind which
I try to shield myself against pedantry and arrogance"[15]—I
suspect something of this sort behind this rhetoric about
"World Spirit" and "ether"). But one thing seems plain to
me: this kind of talk of death as a "return into the ether"
has certainly not passed into ordinary colloquial usage—any
more than countless other phrases which may be found in
philosophical literature, such as, say, Gustav Theodor Fech-
ner's celebrated definition of death as a passing over from a
realm of intuition to a realm of recollection.

All the same, though we confine our stocktaking to the
area of plain everyday language, our results are sufficiently
variegated to startle and perplex us. But after all it is only
logical that the multiple aspects of this theme should be revealed in the multiplicity of linguistic terms for it, in a
plurality which cannot be reduced to a common denominator. Each one of those terms arises from an actual finding
of experience; but each needs to be supplemented by all the
others. Not that each separate name for death and dying
could not be safely considered and spoken by itself; but none
may be isolated from the polyphonic whole, with its full
range of linguistic implications.

We may hazard at least this: our thinking runs afoul of the
human experience embodied in living speech, afoul of reality
itself, as soon as we leave out a single one of the following
aspects: that <u>death and dying mean both end and transition,
both terror and liberation, both something violent and something maturing from within, something happening to us but</u>

also something we ourselves perform, something natural and occurring by nature but at the same time something that runs counter to all natural volition.

Hans Urs von Balthasar[16] once grumbled at how soon ordinary "Christian philosophical anthropology" when "asked the decisive questions" reached "its wit's end". "What tortuous answers we receive when we pose the simple question of whether or not death belongs to the nature of man." But anyone who answered this question with an outright Yes or an equally definite No would be giving, certainly, not a "tortuous" answer, but not an adequate one either. Often a simple answer is a wrong one.

III

What does "Separation of Body and Soul" mean?

THE time has come, after these preliminary considerations of vocabulary, to formulate a reply to the question we asked at the outset: What actually takes place when a human being dies? Now we are no longer concerned with names, but with a description of what happens which will penetrate to the heart of the matter. Still the best thing we can do is to leave aside for the present any profound speculations we may encounter and instead to begin with what people "commonly" say.

That is precisely how Plato's Socrates proceeds in his death cell, on the last day before his execution, when he discusses the question of immortality.[1] He asks his assembled friends to vouch for the fact that everyone understands "something quite definite" by death and dying. What is that? "Nothing other than the separation of soul from body." Plainly, this phrase is not meant to express anything new and original, but rather something to be utterly taken for granted, which no one would seriously doubt. And right up to the present day, it seems, that "understanding" has remained essentially unchanged. The man of our own times may have reservations about the soul as something independent and separable, but he will readily come up with that old phrase as soon as the question is posed. The vital principle "leaves" the body which up to this moment has been animated by it. Even though some may find it more meaningful to say that the body "leaves" the soul, withdrawing from it[2]—even then the process of separation is still viewed as the decisive factor.

This idea also constantly recurs in Christian theology as if it stood in need of no further discussion. We find, for example, Thomas Aquinas saying that the *ratio mortis*, the "concept" of death, implies that the soul separates from the body, *animam a corpore separari*.[3] This definition may not conform to the sacred books of Christendom[4] but at the same time from the first Christian centuries on up to the official pronouncements of the twentieth-century Church it has been, as Karl Rahner[5] puts it, "used so naturally that we must regard it as the classical description of death from the theological point of view". However, Rahner has certain grave reservations: not only is this characterization of dying a mere "description" which fails to define "the real nature of death", but the description itself is problematic "because the concept of separation remains obscure".[6]

This is the point at which, it seems to me, we must begin to think critically. For it is not the formal concept of "separation" which is dubious and "obscure". Separation means the abolition of a connection; there is not the slightest obscurity about that. The question is, rather, what is the nature of the connection which antedated the separation. Two acquaintances meet by chance on the street, converse briefly and "separate". Mother and child, as the Red Cross can daily testify, are "separated" in escaping from a war zone. In an accident an arm or a leg may be "separated" from the body. The concept of separation is always the same, and what it states is transparently clear. On the other hand, what precedes the event of separation in each given case is different; and this lends a different "meaning" to the concept of separation, which in itself does not vary. Thus, if dying consists of the separation of body and soul, the way we understand this event depends, of course, on how we conceive the things which are separated in death to have been connected with one another in life. In other words, the meaning of death depends on the conception we have of man himself and of his physical being.

At this point we must bring up Plato once again; or, more precisely, we should perhaps speak of Platonism and of the Platonists. Plato's own stand, as we shall see, is far more complex and far more fraught with tensions than the "isms" linked with his name would suggest, even though these do indeed derive from him. (But that is a well-known and recurrent phenomenon in the history of thought.) Nevertheless, Plato himself, in order to clarify the connection between body and soul, coined a metaphor which was to be widely although not exclusively accepted in the Western world for more than a millennium and a half after him. There is something in man, he says, which uses the body like an apparatus or a tool; and this something is the soul—we find this stated in, for example, the Platonic dialogue *Alcibiades*, in which the even more consequential statement is made: "The soul *is* the man."[7] In their acceptance of this—we are dealing with one of the firmest findings of the history of philosophy[8]—all Christian thinkers before Thomas Aquinas were "Platonists"; all defined man as the soul which uses the body as the musician his lute. To be sure, in the realm of Christian thought this thesis has never been fully "realized", for it does not accord with some of the fundamental tenets of sacramental theology nor with burial ritual, veneration of martyrs and the belief in resurrection. But in the realm of philosophical reflection there has been broad acceptance of the proposition: *Homo est anima utens corpore*—with which Thomas Aquinas[9] summed up the opinion of Plato. This conception appears to attain to full "realization", to be given the widest intellectual application, only after the Christian sacramental and cultic counterpoises have lost some of their potency. At any rate, Descartes assigns to the idea a comprehensive and systematic significance which it never had in St Augustine's thought. Augustine's philosophical anthropology could never have been characterized by the sentence: "I have my integrity in being a thinking entity—without body"—whereas this is the quintessence of the thought of Descartes.[10] For Descartes man is an "angelic" being of pure spirit which by chance and irrelevantly dwells in a body.[11] Here we have a return to the line of pre-Christian spiritualism—the tendency expressed in Cicero's *Dream of Scipio* ("Be firmly convinced that *you* are not mortal, but this body"[12]) or in Marcus Aurelius's *Meditations* ("Thou art a little soul bearing about a corpse"[13]).

But what all this says about death is easy to show; in fact, it is almost self-evident. *First,* the things that separate in death have from the start been twain and not one. What happens in death is that the artisan lays aside his tool, or lets it drop, and that the sailor steps out of the boat, which he now no longer needs after having landed. What takes place may even be likened to a liberation from a dungeon, the ending of an imprisonment. But the *second* statement is even more important: If body and soul are really two things which have from their origin been separate in essence, and if the soul, it alone, is the "real man", then whatever happens in death is something that does not affect the core of us. Schopenhauer put this in the bluntest way: Man remains, when he dies, fundamentally "uninvolved".[14] Schopenhauer

35

invokes the Platonic image of the body as the instrument of the soul: "Because the spinning wheel stands still is no reason to infer the death of the spinner."[15]

It is perfectly understandable that this spiritualistic minimizing of dying should have provoked a corrective in the form of a realistic doctrine of man, and a counterassault by materialism. I am convinced that the great intellectual movements have never sprung from the arbitrary inclinations of their spokesmen. And it seems to me in any case a highly significant fact that Ludwig Feuerbach, one of the founders and inspirers of Marxist materialism, should have begun his literary career with *Thoughts on Death and Immortality*, in which he quite rightly objected to the pseudo-Platonic as well as pseudo-Christian theology of the Enlightenment on the ground that it had falsified the reality of men's dying into a mere "sham death".

But what is actual, real death? And above all, who is it who dies? The answer to this second question can only be: It is the man, the whole body-and-soul man whom dying befalls; it is he who suffers death; he is affected and involved, with body and soul. This does not mean that the materialistic view is right in saying that man, like any other organism, is entirely extinguished in death—a view which disturbingly enough is nowadays held by certain schools of Protestant theologians, although they base it on entirely different premises. It seems to me that they too are taking this position in reply to the "Enlightened" argument for immortality which in fact reduces human death to a mere semblance. Against this the Protestant theologians even maintain that according to the New Testament "not only the body but also the soul dies".[16]

36

My own position is neither one nor the other. Instead I would uphold the hypothesis, first, that it is not man's body nor his soul which "dies", but man himself; and, second, that the spiritual soul, although profoundly affected by death, connected with the body by its innermost nature and remaining related to it, nevertheless persists indestructibly and maintains itself, remains in being.

Let us then speak first of what death means within the whole of existence, and say that its sovereignty is such that there can be no zone of our beings which remains uninvolved, exempt. Once again, then: "<u>One cannot say that because the soul lives, the body dies but the man lives. The man dies.</u>"[17]

When we speak of a "dying" culture or of "immortal" fame, we all know that the words are being used in an extended, figurative sense. A culture or fame or a poem are not of such nature that the word "dying" can be used of them in a strict sense, any more than "never-dying". But if we take the sense of words in their true meaning and respect the linguistic standards embodied in speech, we cannot say either that the man's body is what dies, or even that the soul also dies. No more can we say that it is the soul's property not to die, but to be immortal. "Die", "mortal", "immortal"—strictly speaking, regarded purely in terms of living language, the only proper subject of this verb and these adjectives is man himself, the whole man composed of body and soul.

Once more, then: *Man dies!* And if there is to be any discussion at all of immortality in relation to man, such immortality in order to be meaningful would have to be attributed not to the "soul", but to the man; we repeat: to the whole man composed of body and soul. And this, surprisingly enough, is actually the language used by the New

Testament. Surprising, at any rate, for those who for whatever reasons have come to consider the doctrine of "immortality of the soul" one of the most essential statements in Christendom's sacred book.[18] In the Bible itself there is scarcely any legitimate grounds for that. The New Testament does not once mention the "immortal soul"; the word "immortality" itself occurs only three times, and then the immortality is attributed not to the soul, but to the risen Christ and the—again bodily—man of the coming eon.[19] What is more, the phrase "immortality of the soul" is strikingly absent from the great theological tradition. Thomas Aquinas, for example, normally does not call the soul "immortal"; he speaks, rather, of its imperishability and incorruptibility. If he does chance to mention "immortality" in connection with man, he has in mind only paradisiacal man[20] or the man of the New Eon who has been resurrected from the dead.[21]

So far, however, we are still speaking of death and dying. What language tells us, that the whole man, and by no means only the body, is affected by death—this information is clearly confirmed by the direct experience of one who shares emphatically in the death of someone close to him. It would never occur to him to think that the dying person, the "real" self within that person, remains fundamentally "uninvolved". And if he had ever believed that death "does not affect the ego", as Fichte says, and that "dying in the temporal world" is nothing but an "illusory phenomenon" to which one "should accord no belief whatsoever"[22]—if he had ever believed such artificial, unrealistic constructs, what he sees of death would in all probability disabuse him.

Even the friends gathered in Socrates' cell obviously do not behave as though they regarded death as the laying aside of a tool. Socrates himself, although he had said "whether I can face death fearlessly is another matter";[23] "I too am not born of sticks or stones"[24]—Socrates goes to his death with superb calm, comparable to the bearing of saints such as Thomas More who asked the executioner if possible not to damage his fine beard. But this intrepidity is nourished by something quite different from the conviction that death does not affect and will not reach the core of existence. It is nourished, as Socrates plainly states, by the hope that on the other side of death there is a place prepared for him in which not mere images of the gods dwell in the temples, but the gods themselves, who will take him, the human being, into a true communion (*synousia*).[25]

But if it is the man who dies, not just the body, but the whole formed of body and soul, obviously there inheres in this description of death, inheres retroactively, so to speak, a √ conception of the inner structure of the human being and his physical existence. That structure, as implicitly contained in such a description of death, cannot be paraphrased by the images of used tools, the sailor in the boat, or the body as the prison of the soul.

And this other conception has likewise been present in the European tradition of thought from the beginning. It was finally expressed by Aristotle, Plato's great pupil, who argued that it is not the soul which is the "real man", but the existential configuration, the unity of soul and body. This thesis has become the model for a broad strand of Occidental philosophical anthropology. When in the course of the so-called "reception" of Aristotle in the thirteenth century, Thomas Aquinas passionately adopted this doctrine and defended it with wholly new, Christian arguments, he knew he was not taking over anything alien, anything Greek and "pagan", but rather recovering a genuinely Christian and in fact biblical idea. *Homo non est anima tantum*;[26] man is not the soul alone. Man is rather by nature (and for Thomas, of course, that phrase means: by virtue of his Creation) a physical being. The body is part of his nature.[27] But given this fundamental concept, not only the man but the soul itself must in a certain sense be termed corporeal. "The soul does not possess the perfection of its own nature except in union with the body."[28]

Since Aristotle this union has been described by a vivid image which points up both the intensity of that union and its (virtual) indissolubility. The soul is connected with the body not like the workman with his tool, nor does it "dwell" in him like the sailor in the boat or the prisoner in his cell; rather it is "in" him the way the stamped form (a coat of arms, a portrait, an eagle) unites with a blank of liquefied silver to make a coin. The form impressing itself on the body from within—that is the true definition of the soul: *anima forma corporis*. "The soul unites with the body not as a sailor with the boat but as its form."[29]

Here, granted, an idea expressed in exemplary form by Aristotle has been taken up. Nevertheless, to repeat, there can be no question of "Aristotelianism". On the contrary, it has been said with complete justice that the great teachers of Christendom would scarcely have dared to espouse the idea of the complete existential unity of body and soul and carry it to its ultimate conclusions had it not been reinforced by the doctrine of the "Incarnation". Strictly speaking, the term means, after all, not "God becoming *man*" but "God becoming *flesh*".

Thomas Aquinas in his *Quaestiones disputatae* once expressed this idea of the existential union of body and soul in

so extreme a manner that the innermost meaning and intention, as well as its ultimately theological basis, emerges with
perfect clarity. One of the hurdles which he himself habitu-
ally placed along the path of thought goes as follows (I
render its meaning faithfully, but somewhat freely and with a
slight reorientation to bring it into line with our present
theme): After death, in the state of bliss, the soul will finally
be liberated from the body, and thereby will be similar to
God, the Pure Spirit. This, as I have said, is the hurdle; it is
the view Thomas *rejects*. This though it comes dressed, as it
were, in the tempting splendour of a highly "spiritual" and
sublime line of argument which will surely impress many
people. But what does Thomas reply: "The soul united with
the body is more like God than the soul separated from the
body, because it possesses its nature more perfectly."[30]
The soul united with the body, then, is not only more
human but also more like God—here is a most aggressive
formulation which seems to defy every form of spiritualistic
theory of man. It is hard to understand how this proposition
by St Thomas should have fallen so entirely into oblivion,
particularly among Christian thinkers, so that modern philosophical anthropology has had to rediscover the idea anew
as something presumably entirely un-Christian, supposedly
contradictory to the Christian view of man's physicality.[31]
Empirical investigation of the structure of human existence,
whether undertaken by depth-psychology or medicine, has
truly confirmed a thousandfold that ancient proposition of
the *anima forma corporis*, and daily confirms it anew—
although, granted, not merely in one sense. That is, these
sciences do not only testify that there is in fact nothing
"purely spiritual" in man, nothing that is thought alone, exclusively intellectual product; rather, there are always ac-

41

companying operations of the senses and functions of the organs. But the statement that the soul forms the body is confirmed by the empirical sciences of man in the other sense too : there is nothing in the human realm which could be called "purely material", purely physical, purely biological (and so on). Rather, organic life in all its dimensions, including the involuntary functions, is partly determined, shaped, "formed" by the spiritual centre of decision in the personality, by free human attitudes towards the world, above all towards the social environment.

Let us for the moment assume that the structural form of physical man and of his earthly existence is indeed *anima forma corporis* and *corpus animā formatum*; that body and soul are not separate realities, let alone locked up together and fettered to one another, at odds with their true natures. Rather, we continue our postulate, both belong together naturally, because of the nature of the soul as well as the body. Both are from their origins amicable and dependent on one another. Not only is the body dependent on the soul, but the soul depends on the body for the unfolding of its life.

If we accept these assumptions concerning the connection by virtue of which man lives as a physical being, certain conclusions follow. We cannot, then, even begin to view the separation of soul and body—that is, dying—as an event which could possibly leave untouched and unmolested any zone of existence whatsoever. Death can no longer be seen as an easy parting of ways between two things that in any case have always been divided and unrelated. Similarly, we cannot regard dying as a process of liberation. Or if we did nevertheless conceive of it as a kind of liberation, then at any rate not liberation from the prison of the body. . . .

At this point a quick warning must be interposed. These words of St Paul in the Epistle to the Romans (7:24), "Who will deliver me from this body of death?" might make us wonder whether there is not, after all, some such dichotomy in Christian tradition. However, these words refer not to the relationship of body and soul, but to the confrontation between "sin and salvation".

But to return to our argument. If body and soul really constitute the single and unitary living man, not only can death not be regarded as a deliverance from imprisonment or even as a merely "neutral" process, but it must be regarded as the violent separation of something that belongs together by nature. It must be called a destruction, a misfortune, a disaster.

It has been said that the pessimistic conception of death is paralleled by an optimistic estimate of the Creation, and *vice versa*.[32] Perhaps that is not an especially felicitous formulation, but it does approach the question in the right way. Those who call death liberation of the soul from the prison of the body in fact proceed from the premise that its incarceration in the body is a misfortune. And as we know, Plato actually described the origin of physical man in a cosmic allegory as the fall of a purely spiritual being into the material body—although he was by no means offering that picture as the final and definitive one.

On the other hand, those who follow the great theological tradition of Christendom and refuse to regard the present state of man and the world as an improper state; those who on the contrary are convinced that all that exists is God's creation and therefore good; that, furthermore, the creature himself, for the very reason that he is a creature, cannot affect the core of his being; those who accordingly refuse to see man's physi-

43

cality as the result of a cosmic misfortune or an angelic or human culpability; those who, rather, see this physicality as something consistent with the Creation, and therefore as it should be and thus entirely good—they must necessarily call the destruction of the body-soul unity which takes place in death a *malum*, an evil, a bad thing, a doom.

If the interrelationship of body and soul really constitutes the existence of the living man, then the dissolution of this unity is *eo ipso* the end of his existence. If the blank of silver loses its stamp, it is no longer a coin. Impressed matter, the block of reality made into a unit by the impress of form, simply ceases to be as soon as the formative factor, the *forma* and the recipient of the form, the *materia*, are parted; or to put this more precisely, as soon as the form loses its power to impress: *desinit esse actu*.[33] In these words Thomas Aquinas is expressing, in the sober terminology of the scholastic, what the language of Scripture puts as follows: "For there is hope for a tree, if it be cut down, that it will sprout again. . . . At the scent of water it will bud. But man dies, and is laid low; man breathes his last, and where is he?" (Job 14:7ff.). In death what is called a "man" simply ceases to exist; "man" in the full and unadulterated sense of the word exists only as a living being.

That is a disturbing finding but one that we can scarcely avoid. In the face of it, language reaches the limit of its denominating powers. For example, we do speak of "the dead man"—but strictly speaking, who can that possibly be? The soulless body, the corpse, is obviously not "the dead man". In Plato's *Phaedo* the practical-minded Crito asks Socrates as he is preparing himself for death what they should do about his burial. Whereupon he receives the magnificently ironic reply: "However you like, provided you can catch me and prevent my escaping you."[34] One element in this answer is incontrovertible: what is to be buried or consigned to the flames is not Socrates.

Thomas Aquinas makes the same point even more incisively in his commentary on Aristotle's *De Generatione et Corruptione*.[35] Strictly speaking, he remarks, it is not enough to say that the physical organism itself no longer remains. Even the limbs of the body must be spoken of in an entirely different sense of the words. To say "flesh and bones" may still be meaningful; but in the strict sense it is no longer possible to speak of a "hand". Only a living, animated hand is really a hand at all.

This is harsh, almost brutal language. But it is forced upon us as soon as we accept the idea, with all its corollaries, that the man exists only in the union of body and soul and that, therefore, once these elements are separated the man no longer exists. Uncannily enough, there no longer exists something that in the strict sense of the word can be called "human".

"Somehow uncanny"—so indeed a modern theologian[36] describes the notion of a soul separated from the body. And C. S. Lewis,[37] speaking of what he calls one of the few facts from which, he says, perhaps the whole of Christian theology might be derived, cites the point that "the dead are uncanny", both the body stripped of its soul and the soul deprived of its body, the "ghost"; "In reality we hate the division which makes possible the conception of either corpse or ghost. Because the thing ought not to be divided, each of the halves into which it falls by division is detestable."

But what then about departed souls? Are they not "the dead"? It is still too soon to come to grips with this question.

Nevertheless, we might notice that traditional Christian theology and theories about man are somewhat wary about using the name "man" in this context,[38] so that Thomas Aquinas,[39] for example, explicitly says that the *anima separata* cannot be called a "person".

In no case, at any rate—so much is clear at the present stage of our investigation—can we imagine that the soul is indestructible in the sense that after death this part of ourselves simply "lives on", "continues to exist". By simply I mean: as if "death mercifully passed it by"[40] and left it untouched. Nowadays we have little tolerance for such formulas by which the reality of death is exorcized away. We can no longer achieve a sham victory over death[41] by such means, no longer hide from ourselves the metaphysical unity of the human person. Such conceits no longer fetch us; we can no longer bring them to our lips. The discoveries of empirical investigation into the nature of man speak too plain a language. The materialistic view might actually seem more credible. I find it highly significant that the "Christian" protest launched by Protestant theology against that idealistic minimizing of death has an almost materialistic cast. But to be sure, neither the one extreme nor the other seems to me to answer.

Nevertheless, here is where we encounter the real difficulty in the way of a contemporary, truly modern analysis of the problem of "death and immortality". On the one hand we must take the arguments of materialism altogether seriously (which does not mean accepting them!) and on the other hand we must not relinquish the truth that the spiritual soul is indestructible.

IV

A Natural Event or a Punishment?

HUMAN death, we have said, represents a destruction, a shattering, something violent and catastrophic: something united by its nature and by virtue of its Creation is parted. This amounts to saying that, from the point of view of the man himself, dying is a senseless break, something strictly opposed to all natural impulse, and particularly to the natural impulse of human consciousness. To that extent, dying is not only not natural, but downright anti-natural.

Here, however, we bring ourselves up short. Can such a statement be made so categorically? Is death really against (man's) nature? We have already remarked that anyone who tried to answer this question with a flat Yes or No would find himself at odds with man's inner experience. On the contrary, we must be ready to encounter an extreme complication at this point. The complication arises out of the matter itself. For of course our understanding of what happens in death brings to a focus all the questions concerning man— not only the question of man's nature, moreover, but also of his history, of the *pathémata anthrópou*, as Plato says: all that has happened to man and all that he has undergone since the very beginning of his historical existence. The reader of Plato's *Symposium* will recall that the words *pathémata anthrópou*[1] are used in Aristophanes' speech on Love. You understand absolutely nothing about the things of Love, he says, if you do not consider what has befallen the human race —by which, as it then turns out, he means principally the

47

primordial fall of man, his loss through guilt of his previous wholeness. The same thing is true of all our thoughts and discussion about death. If we mean to treat of fundamental existential matters, we cannot shirk the task of considering the implicit meanings of such "mythical" tales.

Is, then, death something "natural"? A thing is not necessarily "natural" because it usually and regularly happens. "Death cannot be an evil, for it is something so universal"—this remark by Schiller[2] strikes us as quite plausible at first hearing; but its logic would be sound only if that which happens everywhere and "universally" were also "natural" *eo ipso*. "Natural" means: inherent in, fitting and consonant with nature—in the present case, the nature of man; in other words, consonant with what nature "wants". The question must therefore be phrased: How can death be something natural when all the forces of the human being resist it, when the fear of dying and repugnance for death are patently so natural, too?

There are several possible answers to this which we must set aside. (But whom do we mean by "we"? I reply: Christians, or more precisely, men who live and have their being in the West's tradition of thought. Our discussion, as has already been said, has by now reached a stage where "ultimate" questions are involved and "ultimate" positions must be taken. For otherwise we cannot say anything of substance.) Among the answers "we" can have no traffic with is Sartre's thesis that it is foolish to speak of "natural" or "non-natural" because there is no human nature,[3] for which reason "what must be noted first is the absurd character of death".[4] We might comment, however, that a man can no doubt hold this conviction of the meaninglessness of all

48

factuality without putting it into words, resignedly or with grim determination, scornfully or apathetically; perhaps such an attitude is far more common than we might imagine.

Another view of the meaning of death holds that while the universe at large is quite meaningful, man in his physical life on earth exists in an improper, distorted state which he overcomes and leaves behind only when he dies—so that one might exhort the dying man not to be afraid but to greet death as a deliverance: "You are ceasing to be something which you would have done better never to have become";[5] "we are at bottom something that ought not to be; therefore we cease to be".[6] These last two sentences were written by Arthur Schopenhauer. But for "us" these statements are again altogether unacceptable. On what basis, we must ask, can it be asserted that physical man ought not to be and therefore that death ought to be, is "natural" in that it liberates man's true being? At any rate this interpretation of death, which incidentally is not so remote from Platonism's, is untenable for one who regards man as a physical being by nature and by virtue of his creation. Seen from this viewpoint, dying is not the shattering of a deceptive appearance, nor of a senseless confinement. It is simply the destruction of the real man.

But could not such destruction possibly be natural? That the powers of the body are consumed and exhausted; that the substance of life wears down and wears out; that the blood vessels become hardened, the heart tired (and so on)—is not all this quite natural? Is not dying simply part of the normal course of life for every organism? Max Scheler[7] in his treatise on *Death and Life after Death* quotes the definition of the great zoologist Karl Ernst von Baer: "Things which can die are called living organisms."

Then were not the old Stoics right: "Do not take the thing hard. Put it to yourself as it is in reality: The time has come for matter to dissolve once again into the elements out of which it was composed."[8] This noble attitude towards death continues to impress us—as, indeed, so much about the Stoa does, including its modern following. There is a stalwart manliness in an attitude of seeming indifference towards death, in simply obeying—perhaps even by suicide— "friendly nature's signal to retreat". There is only one problematical aspect about it, one aspect that arouses our distrust: its secret strain, its tenseness. For at bottom it is after all an attitude directed against nature.

The "natural nature" of man emerges far more clearly in the simple, ordinary opinion, taken virtually for granted by most people, that death is not only an evil but the worst thing that can happen to us. It must be added that this opinion, too, can easily be carried to such a radical extreme, made so principled a thesis, that it becomes false. Nevertheless, everyone knows that to wish someone's death does not mean wishing him a good, but wishing him something evil.

This more or less instinctive judgment of the ordinary man is confirmed by theological reflection. "Human death is frightening and mysterious, no matter how plausible it may be scientifically. For death is the downfall of what is bent on life"—thus Hermann Volk.[9] And Romano Guardini in his essay on The Last Things: "Bread is meaningful in itself, as are light, truth, love—human death is not"; "death is neither 'the intimate fancy of the earth' which was how Rainer Maria Rilke saw it, nor Hölderlin's summit of life, nor anything else of that sort. . . . It does not spring from the necessary condition of human existence."[10] The Protestant theologian Oscar Cullmann[11] flatly calls death "un-

natural" and even "abnormal"; from the point of view of ✓
the New Testament, he says, he would "not venture to join
Karl Barth . . . in speaking of 'death as natural'."

Goethe makes many fine phrases on the subject: death is
"the entrance into the ether" or "a trick of life whereby to
enhance itself". But when he is speaking in all seriousness,
with what we might call existential earnestness, he seems to
brush away such literary formulas. Then we may find him
saying he hates to think of all that will be destroyed by his
own death;[12] or that even if life "is no longer worth living"
we are "not so constituted" that we can easily abandon it;[13]
or that it is simply impossible to think of death as possible, it
always appears "as something incredible", as "an impossibility which suddenly becomes reality".[14]

But let us look to the great tradition of Christian theology.
Its pronouncement is unequivocal: "Of all human evils,
death is the worst";[15] it is "the most extreme of all human
suffering";[16] by it man is "robbed of what is most lovable:
life and being".[17] Thus Thomas Aquinas, who in these
strong sentences clearly places himself, it seems to me, on the
same side as Ludwig Feuerbach, the realist and materialist,
and against the kind of idealistic sham which would represent physical death as something unreal. When, to be sure,
Feuerbach goes on to say that there is no remedy for the
evil of death, that no medicinal herb for it can be found
growing anywhere, "not even upon the manure of theology"[18]—Thomas Aquinas would probably not entirely
agree. Still, he too is convinced that death cannot be overcome ✓
by thinking, nor by theological reflection. If it can be con-
quered at all, then only by something real, by life itself.

But the question still remains open: If death is something

non-natural, an evil, something that should not be—then how can it simultaneously have meaning? When his friend's fiancée died, young Hölderlin[19] wrote: "May . . . God forgive me—I do not understand death in His world." The horizon of the question is precisely of this extent.

This is the point to speak of a piece of information offered by the sacred tradition of Christendom—and by other sources as well—which is, for all its distinctness, difficult to understand. It is that something can be non-natural, indeed antinatural, and nevertheless necessary and indispensable within the whole of concrete existence. A loss can be healing; something bad can be good for us for the very reason that it oppresses and torments us. This curious configuration, this association of seeming incompatibles, becomes clear in a single case: in the concept and the reality of *just punishment*. And just this is expressed by the tradition: death has been imposed upon man as punishment.

We all can testify from our own reaction how staggering such an idea initially is to our minds, if we are willing to dwell on it at all and not reject it outright as simply unendurable and outrageous. At bottom we come very close to rejecting the concept of punishment in itself as unacceptable. Nietzsche can well stand for the man of our time when he speaks of the "filth of the words revenge, punishment, reward, requital",[20] and when among his famous "nays" he mentions his assault upon the concepts of "guilt" and "punishment":[21] "My programme: elimination of punishment."[22] Formerly, he says, the idea of "the atoning power of punishment" still carried weight; "punishment purifies; in the modern world it soils".[23] "In antiquity misfortune really still existed, pure, innocent misfortune; with Christianity everything became punishment"[24]—even death. Now as for Nietzsche's picture of "antiquity"—it was, as is well known, a highly romantic one. The concept of death as an act of atonement can, for example, be found in the famous saying, preserved only as a fragment, of the Milesian philosopher Anaximander, two hundred years before Plato: "The source from which existing things come to be is that into which they pass by necessity, for they pay penalty and retribution to each other for their injustice, according to the assessment of time."[25] Plato, too, has Aristophanes in his speech in the *Symposium* explain the whole wretchedness of history as a punishment,[26] the consequence of culpability in prehistoric times—in other words, of a fault not committed by present man himself, but whose consequences he must nevertheless bear.

Still there is every evidence that such notions are repugnant to the modern mind. Not only do we rebel against regarding the total condition of historical man as determined by prehistoric guilt and punishment; in fact, even in our community lives we can no longer accept the concept of "punishment" in its full force, neither ideologically nor in practice. This becomes apparent from any public discussion on reforming the penal code, or from the disputes of educators on the rationale or folly of punishment in education. To be sure, the arguments pro and con are ancient. The theory that the punishment exists not for the sake of atonement, but for the sake of reform, prevention or deterrence, has been present in European thought for thousands of years. Seneca[27] said that punishment is imposed not because a fault has already been committed, but so that no new one will be committed.

Naturally, such ideas are perfectly cogent. But we should be clear on one point: reform, prevention and deterrence are one thing and punishment is another. However, we are now concerned not only with the accuracy of definition and denotation, but with the fact that a measure of deterrence (for example) by which "the affected person suffers a loss"[28] (to quote the legal definition) is absolutely unjust unless it can also be justified as punishment in the strict sense of the word. "What can be more immoral than to inflict suffering on me for the sake of deterring others if I do not *deserve* it? . . . And what can be more outrageous than to catch me and submit me to a disagreeable process of moral improvement without my consent, unless (once more) I *deserve* it?"[29]

What, then, do we mean by "punishment in the strict sense of the word"? We do not, of course, intend to sketch a general theory of punishment here; that is neither possible nor necessary. But it is essential to speak of two elements in the concept, elements which everyone invariably thinks of when he says the word "punishment" in spontaneous, living language.

The first is that in the process of punishment something happens to the affected person from outside, something undesired, bad, evil, something antipathetic to volition—perhaps not only the punished person's volition, but in a sense the punisher's also. *Poena* and *pain* are the same word.

The second, far more crucial characteristic of punishment is its relationship to previous culpability. Punishment is essentially a response;[30] it is by its nature secondary, a consequence.[31] A fault for which the culpable person is responsible must have preceded it; and it must itself, in its quality and quantity, correspond to the extent and nature of the fault. An "unjust punishment" is virtually a contradiction in terms. Punishment is either just or it is not punishment at all. But then what? An outburst of rage, an act of revenge, an act of abuse or violence.

When we analyse these two key elements we instantly see that punishment has to be both at once: something bad which is at the same time just; an evil and nevertheless a good; far less of an evil, in fact, than a good. *Puniri non est malum*;[32] although the punishment pains us and deprives us of a good, and indeed *even as* it does so, it is, viewed as a whole, not something bad but something good.[33]

Naturally this idea must not be carried to extremes, or else we swiftly lose touch with reality. The ancients, at any rate, when contemplating the miseries in the world, saw what is obvious to everyone and called even divine punishment an evil, one that must be accepted and endured, certainly, but not something we are capable of loving as we otherwise love the good.[34] Nevertheless they did explain all the bad things in the world of man that were not faults or sins as being punishments. At least since St Augustine the Western tradition of thought has repeatedly held[35] that in the realm of thinking creatures there are only two forms of evil: guilt and punishment; the evil that we do and the evil that we suffer; the evil that is done by our will and the evil that is done against our will.

There is, they assert, no third possibility. And this is where we feel a bitter thing is being asked of us. This argument above all challenges our sense of justice. Wherever we look, is not the world full of sufferings which strike precisely the innocent? How can such sufferings be punishment? Punishment for what? What about the sufferings inflicted upon children?

We might add many other objections here. But I am not going to try to condone that old distinction. I am far too deeply convinced that we are dealing here with the most enigmatic riddle of existence, for which the better name is probably "mystery". (Neither Augustine nor Thomas Aquinas, incidentally, were in any doubt about that.) Still I would suggest the following line of thought in answer to the objections that throng to mind: Let us for once not speak of the suffering of others, let us for the moment stifle all that we want to say in the face of evil which strikes the innocent. Instead let us attempt to answer two questions.

First question: How have great men responded to evil? By great men I do not mean efficient and successful men, masters of the art of shaping the world to their will. Nor do I mean the scientists and artists of genius. I refer to those who have exemplified true *humanitas*, towards whom we turn for pertinent existential answers—men like Socrates, Francis of Assisi, Gandhi. How have such men taken the evil that has come their way, especially the evil from other men? Is there one among them who branded it as a fundamentally unjust visitation?

Second question: If something bad happens to ourselves, something, be it noted, that really cannot be averted—what, in the depths of our heart, is the "right" response to it? Acceptance or rebellion? Do we not all have some secret knowledge that whatever happens to us is never entirely unjust?

As I have said, I am not going to launch on a formal defence of this concept. But within its compass, the view of human death as a penalty imposed by God clearly occupies a special place; and undoubtedly it has its own dignity, quite apart from the validity of the general thesis concerning guilt and punishment. It is true that the idea of the punitive nature of death requires, as we shall see, closer analysis. Nevertheless, some conclusions can already be discerned.

If death is in truth punishment, then there is something in it that ought to be—something good, that is; at any rate, it cannot be entirely bad—insofar as punishment "makes good again" and restores to order something which had been wrong. After all, one could not say this of guilt; one could not see something good in it. It may be that a culpable fault eventually "turns out well", that it leads to something beneficial, or that, as we say, God turns it to good. In this sense the phrase *felix culpa*, a salutary fault, has been used, and with reason. But in itself the *malum culpae* is something that fundamentally ought not to be; precisely here lies its distinction from *malum poenae*. It is inherent in the nature of the latter that something of good is contained within it, within the punishment itself. To be sure, this good is not brought about of its own accord, and not in every case; it is obtained solely by one who accepts in his heart the *malum,* the badness and bitterness, the punishment.

The badness and bitterness, therefore, absolutely must be seen and "tasted". Death is not a neutral event in nature, and certainly not a liberation of the soul from the imprisonment of the body, but the violent rending of a living unity, the destruction of the real man. The bitterness, the *malum,* the thing in dying that ought not to be, does not reside solely and perhaps not even primarily in the pain and fear that beset man, but above all in the profound wrongness which death signifies to the thinking intellect questioning the meaning of existence, to man as a mind. The thinker lucidly perceives the uttermost bitterness of death only when he feels he is right in saying that "the whole state of things" which result in man's having to die is "not in order".[36] And he is right indeed—since death after all is the consequence of something that ought not to be.

Countless statements could be collected expressing this protest against the incomprehensible, the impossible thing which nevertheless happens day after day. Sigmund Freud[37] expresses it tersely: "<u>At bottom no one believes in his own death.</u>" Karl Jaspers: "We can know death in general and yet at the same time there is something within us which instinctively regards it as not necessary and not possible."[38] Schopenhauer put it this way: "It might be asked how much each man in his heart actually believes in a thing which he cannot really conceive; or whether perhaps . . . our own death does not seem to us at bottom the most fantastic thing in the world."[39] For man, says Jacques Maritain, death is something "not so much frightening as incomprehensible . . . a violation, an insult, an offence".[40] Surprisingly enough, this feeling does not spring solely from the highly differentiated sensibility of the modern intellectual; according to the ethnologists, the Maori of New Zealand employ almost the very same phrases. They, too, regard death as a dishonouring thing that strips man of his dignity.[41]

All this, be it noted, should not be construed to mean that death arouses mere incomprehension. On the contrary, what these statements record is the strong sense that when a man dies something fundamentally untoward is happening, something that cannot have been intended. Moreover, we have here an attitude that goes beyond merely theoretic and as it were academic knowledge and presentiment; we have something akin to protest. Karl Rahner, in fact, uses the word "protest" in this context—although precisely in this context it could be misinterpreted. "Death is the most universal thing," the passage begins in Rahner's essay *On the Theology of Death* (Schiller, we will recall, concluded from this "universality" that death cannot therefore be an evil; but who can subscribe to this view?): "Death is the most universal thing, and every man declares it is natural and a matter of course that one dies. And yet there is alive in every man a secret protest. . . ."[42] Rahner is careful not to represent this protest as simply the expression of the will to live; to see the matter in that light, he says, is to falsify the problem.[43]

The "problem", to put it briefly, is this: Despite all the empirical proofs and arguments to the effect that everything which is born passes away and dies, we remain unswervingly convinced that death for man is not simply something "natural". Rahner[44] holds that the intellectual system of "metaphysical anthropology" cannot explain this contradiction. I agree completely with this opinion, insofar as Rahner is referring to a "purely" philosophical science of man which pits itself against the pre-philosophical "sacred" tradition (although I would be tempted to call that "purely" philosophical approach *un*philosophical). For that very reason I have brought in for consideration the "theological" view which states that human death has the nature of a punishment—a view which appears not only in Christian, but also in non-Christian sacred tradition.

The word "punishment" at once implies: something non-natural. It is simply inherent in the concept of punishment, as well as that of reward, that both are extraordinary, that they fall out of the line of what regularly and normally happens, in keeping with the nature of the thing itself. I cannot very well pay my secretary her regular salary and say that this is at the same time a reward for the special care she has taken during the past month. What applies to reward applies to punishment. The word addressed to Adam in Genesis (2:17), "Thou shalt surely die", would have no point as a threat of punishment, or as Thomas Aquinas[45] puts it, would have been spoken in vain (*frustra diceretur*), "if man by the constitution of his nature were in any case under the necessity of dying".

At this point a very serious objection might be advanced—somewhat prematurely, as we shall see, but still logical enough. The objection is this: Since Adam, men have died without exception. Furthermore, death is evidently a matter deeply affecting man; it is an event which touches the core of existence. If you now assert that death is a punishment and therefore non-natural, not *eo ipso* inherent in the "constitution" of human nature—which is the same as saying that it would not occur unless something had taken place before the first man died, or more precisely, unless something specific had been done—if you say this, then have you not declared that the state of historical mankind is fundamentally and at its very core an improper state? Are you not saying exactly what Platonism, if not Plato himself, asserted: that the state of being of physical man as a whole, that in fact man himself is nothing but the result of a great cosmic misfortune? Are you not likewise saying, like Schopenhauer:[46] "We are at bottom something that we ought not to be; therefore, we cease to exist." Are you not therefore, contradicting yourself, after having explicitly rejected such notions as unacceptable to "us", that is, to Christians who conceive of the world and man as *creatura*? Have you not said: We refuse to believe that the world or man exist in a basically improper state? Rather, we hold that this physical world as we behold it is good because it is Creation. . . . The objection would, I think, be phrased somewhat along these lines.

Obviously the answer to it cannot be simple—if the matter can be threshed out at all.

Let us first consider Platonism's view that the whole condition of man is the consequence of a fault, a transgression that occurred in the very beginning of history. This view, by the way, can appear in the most surprising terminological disguises, even where there is no trace of Plato or—as in the case of Schopenhauer—of Buddha. (Thus I wonder, for example, whether the concept of "alienation", as it occurs in ideological Marxism where it is used in a well-nigh mythological ✓ sense, does not come down to the same thing. Marx in his youth, at any rate, used this term to mean the loss of man's harmony with his true being, which loss moreover is to be attributed to a transgression. To be sure, the question is what kind of transgression and whose?) But to continue : we must probably say that this whole interpretation of the world and existence is wrong, but not without some reason, not without foundation, there is much in man's actual existence that calls it forth. It is an error, but perhaps one that rests upon a deeper insight than does many an orthodox view. The great, inextinguishable heresies usually crystallize, I am convinced, around precisely such kernels of truth. It is scarcely likely that they would have arisen out of a total misconception. Consequently, in the confrontation with such "great" errors the important thing is not at all to "dismiss" them and "refute" them; the important thing is to salvage and preserve the grain of truth contained in them. In fact, the test of real spiritual superiority has always been the ability to do just that.

Nevertheless, there can be no compromise with the thesis that man exists in a basically improper state. Above all it is) too simple to do justice to the multiple aspects of the matter. We refuse, therefore, to accept the interpretation that the total condition of man is an outright contradiction of his origins, an alienation from his true being, a degeneration. But, it may

61

be objected, aren't you actually doing that yourself, exactly that—for you plainly say that man must die because of a fault incurred, whereas before. . . .

At this point I would interrupt my interlocutor and ask him to recall the entire argument. The reason for my position, my refusal to accept the thesis of man's life as an improper state, is precisely that we are trying to sustain the idea of the universe as Creation. Inherent in this idea are two others: First, that everything that is is good, and that it is good to be —and this for no other reason than because everything real, in that it has entered into existence, is desired and affirmed by the *Creator*. We love things because they are; but they are good because God loves them.[47] Secondly, inherent in the concept of Creation is the idea that the *creatura*, that is to say, a being receiving its own existence entirely from outside, can never by itself effect a fundamental change in its own state of being and its own existential goodness—not even given the premise of freedom and the possibility of misusing this freedom to oppose the divine purpose. Man is, in that and because he is *creatura*, absolutely incapable of remodelling his created being, his "nature", either for good or evil, even if he were to desire passionately to do so (and probably even such desire is itself impossible). No fault, no crime, no matter how "inhuman", can so profoundly change man that he could ever cease to be really human, with all the natural endowments that belong to man: spirituality, physicality, personality—and so on.

Here, then, lies the decisive difference from the world view of Platonism (for example). The Platonic version, as expounded in the dialogue *Phaedrus*, is as follows: that because of a primordial fault a being of pure spirit, an "angel", fell into the material world and thus become a man—or rather, that in this way "man" as a whole originated. In other words, man himself, as he exists today, a being of body and soul, was not actually meant to be! But this is an absolutely unthinkable thought for one who conceives the world and man as *creatura*. The Christian, on the other hand, is convinced that at the beginning of man's history there was a primordial transgression which ever since has profoundly influenced the destinies of man and will continue to influence them. This is not to believe that man before the first sin was not man just the same. One might venture to say that man became "different" because of that primordial transgression. But it is surely impossible to say that he became "something different".

However, this very formulation could kindle the dispute anew, and make it even hotter than before. To be changed from an immortal being to a mortal one—is that not "becoming something different"? Or else, is that not what is meant when it is said that death was imposed upon man as a punishment. The answer to this question can only be: No, that was not meant! As I have already said, the objection as a whole has been raised somewhat prematurely, for our definition of the punitive nature of human death should first have been phrased with greater precision. What, then, does this definition mean? I shall anticipate the gist of the answer by quoting Thomas Aquinas. The quotation states that the proposition of death as a punishment is valid, but does not express the whole of the matter. Thomas says in the *Summa theologica*:[48] *Mors et est naturalis . . . et est poenalis;* death is both something imposed as a punishment and something natural. Would this mean that death is in one respect natural, in another respect non-natural? Indeed, it means just that.

Thomas[49] himself formulates the idea this way: *Mors quodammodo est secundum naturam et quodammodo contra naturam*, "death is in a certain sense according to nature and in a certain sense contrary to nature". We shall have to keep this forceful phraseology in mind.

In any case, the time has now come to speak in greater detail of *both* aspects of the interpretation of death, and above all, of course, of how these two contradictory aspects can conceivably be paired.

If we consider first of all the non-naturalness of death, its contrariness to nature, its punitive character, the question that inevitably arises is: punishment for what and why? To which the sacred tradition of Christendom replies with the biblical story of the first sin. To the two quotations from Thomas Aquinas cited above I might add a third which directly links his doctrine of death with the primal sin: *Necessitas moriendi partim homini est ex natura, partim ex peccato*, "the necessity for man's dying derives partly from nature, partly from sin".[50]

At this point I am prepared for a critical interjection: Well then, will we from now on be engaged in theology? This question has often been flung at me and I am deeply concerned to make it plain that the answer is, "No". No, we are not engaging in theology; or at any rate not when, in attacking the problem of death in a philosophical way, which is to say under every conceivable aspect, we consider what we believe about the theme of death and include the theological interpretation of that belief in our considerations —doing so, moreover, frankly and expressly, with our cards on the table. No one who engages in philosophy with existential seriousness can omit this branch of thought, no matter whether *in concreto* he is considering the creeds of atheism (as with Jean-Paul Sartre) or of Hinduism (as with Radhakrishnan) or Christianity. Of course it matters very much what the creed and the religion offer in their defence. But still this play of what a man knows against what he believes must be performed with critical keenness; otherwise we would no longer be considering the subject at hand under every conceivable aspect, which is the same as saying we would no longer be philosophizing.

The theologian, on the other hand, has an entirely different task. His business, to put it in a nutshell, is to study the documents of a sacred tradition for their true meaning And that is something we are by no means doing here.

Instead, what we are really doing is the following: Concentrating on the phenomenon of human death, as we meet it in our inner and outer experience, and inquiring into the ultimate meaning of this phenomenon, we deliberately summon up what sacred tradition, according to the theological interpretation of that tradition, has to say on the subject. We summon up, that is, the following item of information : that there is something in death which entered into it because of an original sin, and that this "something" is not only non-natural but contrary to nature.

Granted, it remains true and uncontested that there exists no complete experience of what really happens when a man dies. If such experience does exist for the dying person, it is neither communicable nor examinable. Nevertheless, the aspects of the phenomenon of death that do fall within our experience are certainly not nothing!

"Experience"—we mean the word here in the sense of an awareness which results whenever and however we ourselves come into direct contact with reality, the reality of the world and also the reality which we ourselves are. But the subject of such experience is the whole man, the physical and mental person with his undiminished—though ever-variable, depending on receptivity and momentary state—sensibility—for which reason so strict an empiricist as Alfred North Whitehead has insisted that "in order to discover some of the major categories under which we can classify the infinitely various components of experience, we must appeal to evidence relative to every variety of occasion",[51] not omitting the experience of the sleeper, the drunkard, the sick man, the frightened man, the enthusiast, and so on.

Thus, while not averting our eyes from what can be and is experienced in the phenomenon of death, we also pay heed to what the sacred tradition has to say concerning this same phenomenon. We add these data to what we ourselves have seen, and consider both—interested above all in whether and how what we have learned by "hearing" coincides with what we have learned by direct observation, whether both converge towards a single answer. Yet we know all the while that there is no reaching that answer or reducing it to a handy formula.

The statement that death has been imposed as punishment and hence must be seen in relation to a primordial transgression, to an ancient sin—this theological statement, too, obviously does not lie entirely outside our experience. To be sure, we have direct knowledge that something like guilt exists, and we also know what, fundamentally, sin is. That we have the capacity to turn away, in clear consciousness and on the basis of a free decision, from what we know to be the true meaning of our life—this is an inescapable fact about ourselves. "Sin" is just that, that alone. "Sin" in the strict sense is not any kind of misdemeanour, violation, infraction of rules; it is the deliberate turning away from God, although it may manifest itself in a thousand concrete forms. I do not think there is anyone who needs to be instructed about that from outside; everyone knows that such conduct lies within human and hence within his own potentialities. But our experience tells us more than that. We know by all sorts of tokens that the reciprocal psychological correspondence connecting the fact of "sin" with the reality of death is not altogether alien to human experience, at least not to man's latent experience. By latent experience I would understand an unspoken awareness, as it were not yet admitted to one's own consciousness, which comes to light when a particular fact, unexpectedly appearing, does not surprise us. It may happen, for example, that someone we are familiar with suddenly fails or proves himself in an exceptional situation. Most of his acquaintances regard his behaviour as startling and incomprehensible. But among the many who know him there will be two or three who may not have expected him to act thus and so, but who perhaps to their own astonishment are not really surprised—because in their daily association with this person they have "seen" something, without actually realizing they have seen it, which now proves to be "experience" with the person.

Can we not, in similar fashion, draw conclusions from a latent experience with the reality of death—from the fact that the tie between culpability and death is fundamentally not so surprising to us? In some way we "know" both elements of this equation. That death is the atonement for a fault—this was early said by Anaximander. Nor, obviously, are men entirely unaware that a gravely culpable act is in itself something deadly, something that merits death.

I recall, from a semester spent lecturing in America, a

long nocturnal conversation with a colleague at the university, an empiricist in the social sciences, a highly cultivated and cosmopolitan person who had retained that admirable American openness (which is largely unknown or virtually banned in German academic circles) in regard to what we might call the dimension of the absolute in life. Our conversation chanced to come round to the traditional distinction between "mortal sin" and "venial sin". My colleague—I do not know whether or not he was a Christian—found the phrase "mortal sin" extremely astonishing, as though he were consciously encountering it for the first time. I wanted to say something in explanation, but he checked me, indicating that he wanted to try to find a plausible interpretation of this curious phrase for himself. And then, after threshing it out a bit he said with great earnestness that it was true, there must actually be something of the sort, misdeeds after which one no longer wished to go on living. I feel that he struck right to the heart of the matter.

The basic shortcoming of all human penalties is their inevitable failure to achieve what our sense of justice demands: correspondence between the punishment imposed and the act to be made good and atoned for. What does the payment of a sum of money have to do with an ugly insult, or years of imprisonment to do with the killing of a man? It is this incommensurability which makes us wonder how death can be a just punishment for sin—until suddenly we become aware that in this case, and perhaps in this case alone, crime and punishment are in complete accord; that death is not, like all human penalties, something imposed more or less without relation to the fault, but is the consequence and fruit already implied in the sin. It is inherent in the nature of sin to be not only something that psychologically merits

68

death, but something that is mortal in itself. Correspondingly, it has been said of death that it is "primarily the expression and the mode of appearance of the essence of sin in the physical being of man".[52] And when traditional theology calls ultimate rejection "eternal death"—in opposition to "Eternal Life"—it is not using a figurative expression. Incidentally, not even this extremest of punishments, the *poena damni*, should be viewed as something simply imposed from outside. Rather, it represents the meting out of the very thing the will itself has chosen when it commits mortal sin: separation from God. So that, if we were to conceive of such extreme punishment as somehow like a prison, we should visualize it as not barred from outside, but from within.

However, we are speaking now of earthly, physical death and its relationship to man's primal sin. But this relationship strikes me as so little external that we can actually say: one who has not recognized the fundamental fatality of sin has not yet seen the true countenance of death.

Here the objection already formulated arises once more: Does not all this mean that man "before", before that "first sin" (whatever may be understood by that) must have been different, not subject to death, at least not subject to it in the same way as now? Is all this not tantamount to saying that man originally, "in the beginning", must have been *immortal*?

It should be clear that we are deliberately assuming a passive role in this argument. Our intent is only to listen and take note of what has been said elsewhere. We are still considering the information embodied in the sacred tradition of Christendom. Thomas Aquinas attempted to render this information in the already cited (and at first glance perplexing) anti-thetical sentence from the *Summa theologica*: on the one hand and in a certain respect, *partim, quodammodo,* death comes to us because of sin and therefore as something imposed as punishment, but on the other hand it is nevertheless, in a certain respect, something inherent in human nature. The question is what exactly is meant by this second aspect and how it can be linked with the first without contradiction.

Obviously (*first*) there must be something in human death as it happens "now" which was not there "before"; otherwise it would not be possible to speak meaningfully of a punishment. This imposition of punishment "afterwards", so says the doctrine, the *necessitas moriendi*, the overwhelming necessity of dying which comes to us from outside, the violent rending asunder of body and soul which we must simply undergo and suffer—this was *not* the way it was "in the beginning". Paradisiacal man was free of it.

But that does not mean (*secondly*), the theological interpretation continues, that man before the original sin must have been immortal *by nature*.[53] If he had possessed immorality by virtue of his own nature, he could not have lost it, not even by sin, any more than the fallen angel, the demon, lost his.[54] Rather, from the beginning the *posse mori*, the ability to die, belonged to the natural constitution of man, including paradisiacal man. The account in Genesis, therefore (*thirdly*), should not be taken to mean that but for the primal sin man's physical existence upon the earth would have been unending. However, the biblical account does speak here of a special gift. Now it is inherent in the concept of gift that one does not possess it outright, and also that one cannot demand and claim it. The gift would have consisted in the spiritual soul's having so effectively infused the body

with its formative power, and thus made it alive, that this
body-soul unity would not have dissolved against man's will.
The end of earthly man would have been a " 'death' without
death", a "pure, manifest, active completion . . . from
within".[55] But such a "deathless death", although a free gift,
would at the same time have been far more in keeping with
the true nature of man as body-and-soul; it would have been
"natural" in a far higher degree than what now awaits
historical man at the end of his life.

Where, then, do we stand in regard to the "naturalness"
or "non-naturalness" of death? The answer, it seems, has
meanwhile become a whole dimension more difficult. And
in fact, in order to define more precisely what is "natural" to
man, we shall have to make several further distinctions, even
as we realize that our conceptual apparatus may be too crude
to see us through the question.

It lies in the nature of man, we have said, that the spiritual
soul confers form and pattern from within upon the matter
organized as body: *anima forma corporis, corpus animā
formatum*. Therefore anyone who speaks of the nature of
man is always dealing with two things: with soul and body.
Consequently, in regard to man the idea of "natural" likewise has two aspects: in keeping with the makeup of the soul
and in keeping with the makeup of the body. And the question is whether both are equally "natural" to the man himself, a being of body and soul. Undoubtedly it is as natural
to us to grasp the reality of the world by conceptual thinking
as to eat and drink. But can it be said that the one activity is
in keeping with our nature, our being and therefore ourselves
in the same way and to the same degree as the other? Obviously not. It becomes evident that there are gradations and

differences of degree in the concept of "naturalness", or at any rate in the realization of that concept. "Because the *forma* determines being in a higher mode than the *materia*, therefore what corresponds to the nature of the *forma* is also natural in a higher measure (*naturalius*) than what corresponds to the nature of the *materia*"—so Thomas Aquinas declares in the *Quaestiones disputatae de malo*;[56] this statement is to be found in the same *articulus* which discusses the question of whether death is something natural.

If we regard the matter organized in the human body, matter which by its nature always remains dissoluble into its elements, we shall have to call death a completely natural process.[57] "Dust you are and to dust you shall return" (Genesis 3.19). The essence of the soul, however, consists in being the vital principle of life. Its whole energy aims at making the body it has patterned and imbued with form alive, and keeping it alive—so that death, considered in terms of the essence of the *soul*, could never be called simply natural.[58] Yet death can only be called outrightly unnatural or contrary to nature insofar as in it the forming of the body is violently interrupted and destroyed contrary to the innermost intention of the soul and of the man himself. Precisely this is what is meant by the *necessitas moriendi* imposed as punishment for the primal sin. The soul loses the power of effectively immunizing the body against corruption;[59] it loses that gift of paradisiacal deathlessness in which the purpose and potentiality[60] of its nature has been fully realized.

This is, as we see, a fairly subtle doctrine whose complexity might easily arouse impatience. But apparently any clarification cannot be had more "cheaply". Even so, it seems, quite a few questions still remain open. If, for example, it is truly the nature of the soul to form and vitalize the body—

how then is man not "by nature" immortal? I can perfectly well imagine theology's answer to this question. Theology would remind us that sacred tradition, both Christian and extra-Christian, never tries to communicate a systematically rounded picture of reality or of man—neither a cosmology nor an anthropology. Rather, sacred tradition speaks of what has actually happened, or still remains to happen, which leads to salvation or catastrophe. What has really happened, theology relates, was that the gift of paradisiacal deathlessness was conferred on primordial man, who then lost that gift through some culpable act. But as to what might have been or might have happened on the basis of man's "purely natural" constitution—concerning this the sacred tradition remains silent.

On the other hand, we must concede that every single element in that complicated theological story is readily borne out by our own "polyphonic" reaction—which likewise has strong elements of paradox—to the phenomenon of death. Thus it is not vain speculation to speak of (admittedly non-existent) "paradisiacal man"; similarly it can prove highly illuminating for the philosopher to consider the (of course *purely* theological) thesis that Christ necessarily had the potentiality for dying, because he was really a man, but that he was nevertheless not subject to the *necessitas moriendi*; Christ died not because he had to but because he wanted to.[61] Hence the being-able-to-die, the *posse mori*, did not first enter the human world through sin. And according to Christendom's theological doctrine of death even this compulsion to die, although imposed as punishment, does not change or damage the essence of human nature—so that we need not be too surprised to find that, for example, Thomas Aquinas[62] after all suddenly finds altogether comprehensible and accept-

able the idea of the ancient Stoa that death is not punishment
at all, but nature; *mors est hominis natura, non poena.*

I said above that men's instinctive reaction, in ordinary
speech, is fully in accord with this many-faceted interpretation of death within the whole of existence. However, the
same cannot be said about the attitudes arrived at by the
operation of the intellect. Here the likelihood of a wrong or
inadequate answer is all too present. To be sure, there is
room for any number of differing accentuations, but to be
valid, they must do justice to the phenomenon of death in
all its aspects. Nothing must be excluded or glossed over.

Thus there is the one pole of forcing oneself not-to-think-
about-it, an attitude fraught with self-deceit. The other pole is
represented by the serenity of the saint who, asked what he
would do if he learned that he would die suddenly during the
next hour, replied: he would continue to play ball. There is
an attitude which simply accepts death as something natural,
something that happens like the greening and withering of
plants or the change of seasons. This attitude, however, is
possible for man only so long as he instinctively regards himself as a part of a vital whole which in fact does not itself
die and remains unaffected by the individual's death. But
the more consciously man lives as an individual, the less is he
capable of ignoring death. So that I find it a highly suspect
matter, to be regarded with considerable mistrust, when this
"primitive" viewpoint establishes itself at the level of critical
consciousness—in the form, say, of metaphysical materialism, or of proletarian class ideology,[63] or of ideological evolutionism.[64] All three have in common the view that the
individual person, and the fact of his being doomed to death,
seem virtually unreal and at any rate totally uninteresting

by comparison with the great historical or evolutionary process for which the problem of death actually does not exist. The more the individual is conscious of his personality, the more natural is it for death, not the concept but the reality, his *own* inescapably impending death, to seem to him a destructive event, something not only frightening but also and above all senseless, an insult and a scandal.

This existential response of outrage, this reaction of mutiny and rebellion against the Creation as a whole, which may lead all the way to an avowal of the absurdity of both death and life—this all-too comprehensible reflex can, it would seem, be at once aired and overcome in only one way. There are tricks, of course, intellectually unclean ways of evading the issue—for example, pretending blindness, refusing to see, overhasty conciliations. These are well known; there is no need to go into them. But no one should seek to purchase concord with God and the world at that price; on this, the nihilists are quite right. The only honest and clean way not to sweep the scandal of death under the rug and on the other hand not to fall into a state of revolt against Creation consists in coming to see death as *punishment*, and submitting to that; once more, not death as an "idea" and general phenomenon, but our own death and the death of those we love.

Let us examine this more carefully. Obviously there can be an assortment of typical reactions to the fact of "punishment", but only one of these reactions is meaningful. An example chosen at random shows this. Suppose, then, that a mother punishes her child by withholding an apple which was intended for his dessert. We are assuming that she is a sensible and just mother who knows something about raising children, and that she is not being harsh to the child out of anger or ill humour. Rather, for a deliberate fault she has imposed a just punishment—indeed, only if it is just can it properly be called punishment.

Possibly the child will simply cry at being deprived of a pleasure and will fail to see any meaningful relationship to his own fault. But perhaps he will comprehend that the withholding of the apple has something to do with the wrong he himself committed. Nevertheless he refuses to acknowledge this connection; that is, he is not just unhappy, but angry, furious. His rage may be directed against his mother or more or less diffusely against the world as a whole, this world which is set up in so beastly a way. Along with refusing to accept the punishment at all he may possibly choose the highly intelligent course of reinterpreting the imposed evil and taking it as a good. ("So I'm not to have an apple? Oh, that's fine, I didn't want one today anyhow; I've had all I want to eat.") I have called this an "intelligent" procedure; of course that is true only in the sense that a deceptive ruse, which perhaps also serves for self-deception, can be called intelligent; viewed in terms of the Whole and in reality, it is distinctly stupid.

Finally we must speak of still another typical reaction to the fact of "punishment"—a reaction which, however, is beyond the powers of a child, for which reason we may drop our example at this point.

One who is about to receive a punishment may possibly speak in the following way: What is happening to me is in fact an evil, something bad, dreadful, a nuisance, a misfortune; but I cannot conceive it as in any way related to a previous fault on my own part. Since, however, a blind and sinister fate governs this world, and since the idea of complaining is repugnant to me, I shall accept the inevitable without making any attempt to gloss it over by interpretation and without drugging myself to make it more tolerable. I shall accept it in full freedom; or rather, no, I shall not accept it but *choose* it, I shall take it myself and thus set my own sovereignty against the tyranny of the one who, as is said, imposed that evil as a punishment.

We need only at this point replace "that evil" by our title word, "death"—and at once the startling pertinence of the attitude described above comes to light. It has been claimed that this is in truth the only decent position for man, this "resoluteness" which "hands itself down to itself, free for death in a possibility which it has inherited and yet has chosen", and in which existence "free for its death", assures itself "the power of its finite freedom", a "freedom towards death . . . certain of itself, and anxious". These phrases, as the reader has probably surmised, are quotations from the work of Martin Heidegger.[65]

With the help of the quotations above, a fine manifesto can be drafted which heroically defies the traditional picture of death. The necessity to die is no longer to have the charac- ✓ ter of something imposed from elsewhere; rather, man is exhorted to prove his autonomous freedom by "choosing" death in advance, "anticipating" it. Undoubtedly there are a good many reasons for the far-reaching influence of this idea. One reason, probably, is the sheer radicality with which Heidegger, in his analysis of everyday life, shatters the reassuring references to "people" dying (other people, that is) and calls the naked dreadfulness of death by name, summons it up before our eyes. But a good part of the attraction rests, I think, simply on an error, on the completely false impression that this appeal to freedom and human pride at one blow triumphantly does away with gloom which, it was assumed, surrounded the old view of death as a punishment. In fact just the opposite is the case. Heidegger does, to be sure, unsparingly point out that aspect of death which makes it a punishment: that is, that it is a dread nemesis which nobody escapes. Yet his doctrine conceals and denies that death is punishment. And as a result dying becomes an abyss of darkness which no ray of light can illumine. On the other hand, it is inherent in the concept of punishment that it makes up for the fault, that it "makes *good* again", and therefore that it is meaningful and even good. But let us leave aside this aspect for the present. Let us speak only of an aspect pertaining more to the formal logic of the matter: that all punishment, because it is a corrective, is inherently non-final; more than that, it is explicitly temporary, an expedient; there is in fact something accidental about it. Punishment by its nature, that is, cannot have been "intended so" from the beginning.

Let us then consider the alternatives. On the one hand a forced, sombre "resoluteness" desperately attempting to choose freely that death which it regards as man's fate because of the inexorably grim nature of the cosmos. On the other hand an interpretation of life—not an arbitrary interpretation or one invented by any individual—which regards the human *necessitas moriendi* as a punishment. If we compare these two views, we can only see the latter as absolutely radiant, a supreme testimony to hope and light.

If we look back on the series of attitudes described so far, we realize at once that none of these reactions accepts the punishment as what it is; none understands and accepts it as punishment. But if it is true that the punishment is something meaningful and good (and in fact that is even said of death: "Insofar as it is a just punishment, death in a certain respect has the character of goodness . . ."[66])—if this is true, then it must also be true that each of these attitudes prevents the person affected by the punishment from receiving the good which was intended for him and for the sake of which the punishment was imposed. That is, in none of these cases is the meaning of punishment really brought out. The mere fact that the punishment actually "takes place" and is simply carried out does not in itself make it meaningful. Everyone can see that the aim of imprisonment, for example, is not accomplished merely by the fact that the prisoner "does time" for the prescribed number of years (which once again, viewed from still another aspect, makes clear the perhaps unavoidable dubiousness of all punishments imposed by men on other men). Thus theology, too, has always insisted that although death has been imposed as punishment in general, the mere fact that someone dies a "natural" death does not in itself (unlike the case of the martyr!) possess "atoning" force, does not make amends, "make good".[67]

We must ask, therefore, what is the right existential response to the fact of "punishment". What is needed to bring about this response; what is the response like; what is presupposed and implied in it? Under what conditions can we manage to receive the "good" that our dying is meant to bring us, the good that is contained in the element of punishment and is therefore painful, agonizing, opposed to our own will, imposed upon us from elsewhere (and so on)?

The first and decisive prerequisite is evidently that we see our own culpability, in which the primal sin is continued and corroborated, and without which there never would have been punishment at all. We must recognize our guilt, acknowledge it—and reject it. Probably the one is impossible without the other; as long as I identify with my guilt, I have not yet recognized it. There is an astonishing sentence in Simone Weil[68] about that: "We experience good only by doing it. We experience evil only by refusing to allow ourselves to do it, or, if we did it, by repenting of it." The "good" inherent in just punishment can, therefore, be received only by one who is able to wish he had not committed the transgression which preceded it.

Furthermore, the concept of punishment always implies someone who by virtue of his powers imposes the punishment. When we have said that death and the necessity of dying are the fruit, the direct manifestation of "mortal" sin itself, are so to speak the "visibility of guilt",[69] we say this only to point up the incomparable rightness—never otherwise attainable, nowhere else to be encountered—of this punishment. This does not mean, however, that death is the automatic consequence of sin in the same sense that an accident may be called the consequence of careless behaviour. Such an accident, too, might also be called a "punishment"; but then the word is being used improperly. Punishment in the strict sense exists only if it is imposed and meted out by authority—whether that authority is the father, the judge, or God himself. To accept a punishment as such means acknowledging the authority of the punisher, and subordinating oneself to it.

One who thus freely accepts a punishment he has recognized as just does nothing which sullies his honour. This has been repeatedly stated in the philosophical doctrines of justice from Plato to Hegel—although it has just as frequently been rejected as an outrageous absurdity by the sophistical theoreticians of human autonomy. Socrates, for example, insists to his angry interlocutor's face that the guilty person is less unhappy as soon as he is punished.[70] And Hegel states that the lawbreaker is actually being "honoured" by just punishment as "a rational being",[71] insofar as the punishment basically is "the consequence . . . of his own will"[72] and the "restoration of freedom".[73]

If then, in our somewhat primitive example, the mother really and justly withholds the apple, it would accrue to the child's good fortune and psychic health if he did not pretend at all but took the punishment for what it is and is meant to be, a bitter experience, while at the same time accepting and enduring this bitterness as a way to make up for his previous naughtiness (which he now recognizes for what it is) and wipe it out once and for all. Possibly the result of this attitude would be that the punishment really, without forcible self-deception, loses its bitterness, at least partly so.

And if, then, the necessity for men to die is really something that can and must be called punishment in the strict sense of the word, perfectly related to and in keeping with the previous fault, imposed on the basis of the most legitimate power imaginable—then in attempting to find the proper existential response to it, man can do nothing more meaningful and nothing more healing and saving—in the most literal sense of the word—than think of the badness of death in conjunction with the still greater badness of the previous fault, and freely submit to the punishment, without attempting to mitigate the thing with this or that misrepresentation. Such conscious acceptance—which would have to be more than an act of the intellect, would have to engage the full energy of man's being—might in truth bring about precisely what the refusal to accept, the rebellious "freedom towards death" of which we spoke above, pretends to achieve. In short, what has been imposed and disposed, what seems merely something to be suffered, might truly be transformed into something freely chosen, so far as is humanly possible—but chosen without all the fierceness and gloom of false heroics; chosen rather under the very human auspices of stout-hearted cheerfulness of soul, that *hilaritas mentis* which has always been the best proof that an act is right, proper and legitimate.

"So far as is humanly possible"—this reservation continues to hold and must be considered. For in no human act of dying, not even the acquiescent or sought-for death of the martyr, is the brutal factuality of the process ever completely annulled by the freedom of acceptance and sacrifice. There is only one death, one single death which was entirely an act of freedom, though it took the form of a cruel execution; only one death in which even the smallest element of *necessitas*, of nature's inevitability, was seared away by the flame of the will. But "only a Man who . . . served in our sad regiment as a volunteer . . . could perform this perfect dying".[74]

V

The *Status Viatoris*

In discussing the acceptance, and the possible non-acceptance, of one's own death, we have brought out something new, an aspect of dying, everyone's dying, which has hitherto gone unconsidered. We are referring not to attitudes towards death in general, or the death of others, or even the death which some day in the distant future awaits us too. Rather, we are concerned with decisions which, it seems, help to determine the event of death itself at its core and confer its true meaning upon it from within. This idea is new insofar as it reaches far beyond the definition of dying as the separation of soul and body, which is the only definition we have so far discussed. It raises questions which evidently can no longer be comprehended by such a description.

In saying this we are of course not gainsaying the view of the end of physical man as the separation of soul and body. That cannot reasonably be doubted. Nor are we denying that this objective event happens to the dying person from outside, so to speak; that it comes upon him and is inflicted upon him like a natural process obeying its own laws. As far as that event is concerned, it does not matter whether death is viewed as natural or as imposed in punishment. Clearly it cannot be said that the will or the ego, in short, we ourselves, ever could administer or accomplish the separation of soul and body. That is just as inconceivable as that we should be able to forestall it. And surely dying can never be described in such language as Goethe[1] used in speaking of the death of

Christoph Martin Wieland: "The reigning chief monad
. . . has dismissed its former subjects from their faithful ser-
vice." Strictly speaking, not even the suicide separates his
soul from his body when he kills himself. He initiates the
process of separation, he starts it going, he induces it. But
the process itself, the actual event of dying, "happens" to
him—perhaps only an infinitesimal moment after the fatal
shot. And even though the phrase is that he "takes his own
life", in reality death "comes upon" him in the same way it
does on someone who dies of old age on his sickbed.

All this, as I have said, remains undisputed. Nevertheless,
along with this objective event of the separation of body and
soul there is evidently something else happening when a
man dies, happening in the midst of the process or alongside
it or beyond it, something altogether different, definitely not
a process of nature but rather something akin to a personal
act, a decision.[2] One might say that a man's end does not only
"happen" but that the man himself "makes an end of it"—
and does so not insofar as he is an object, a part of nature, but
insofar as he is a subject, a someone, a spiritual person, which
means a being not only capable of and called to free decision,
but also one who cannot avoid such decision.

But the end of a man's own existence which, as we have
said, the man himself is agent of (within the natural event of
separation of body and soul over which he has no control)—
this is likewise a real termination; it is so definitively termination that it seems far to exceed that separation in its finality.

The tradition has coined a formula for this personal sealing
of earthly existence. It is described as the termination of the
status viatoris.

Viator means wanderer, walker, wayfarer, pilgrim. The
last term has acquired a special meaning and become a

familiar part of religious parlance. We speak of the "pilgrim-age" of this earthly life. This is a perfectly honourable and legitimate use of the word, to which no serious objections can be raised. However, certain rather melodramatic over-tones have become associated with this usage, overtones which may blur the precise meaning of this important term, or even cause us to brush it aside. In reality the concept of *status viatoris* involves nothing sentimental, nor even any-thing distinctively religious or theological. What is meant, rather, is that man, as long as he exists in this world, is characterized by an inward, as it were ontological quality of being on-the-way to somewhere else. The life of historical man is structured as becoming, "not-yet", hope. Granted, we have countless choices on our "life's journey". We can make detours and take byways; we can stand still; perhaps also we can, in a certain sense, go backward. Above all we can progress in the true direction. Only one alternative is barred to us, that of not being *en route* at all, of not being "on the way". This quality of man's "being as becoming" has been treated extensively in modern philosophical anthropology, especially in the existential camp—starting with Pascal ("We are not, we hope to be"[3]) and going on to Gabriel Marcel, Ernst Bloch and Jean-Paul Sartre. Marcel's philosophical and dramatic works present a multitude of variations on the fundamental insight that hope is the stuff of which our soul is made.[4] And Sartre strikes precisely the same note when he says that our life is "made up not only of waitings but of waitings which themselves wait for waitings".[5] As for Ernst Bloch's fascinating though rather perplexing philosophy of hope and the future, it certainly makes one point with complete clarity: "The real thing, in man as in the world, is impending, waiting";[6] man is something "not yet at all present, and for that very reason he has history."[7]

As we have said, this is precisely the meaning of the traditional phrase *status viatoris*; it denotes the dynamic state of not-yet-being, of still unfulfilled and incomplete being that is, however, pointed towards fulfilment, completion and final realization. Incidentally, one can come to this perception without overmuch philosophical speculation. It is accessible to everyone on the basis of ordinary empirical knowledge, on the basis of experience with himself. No man has ever said: I have already completed the draft which I myself am; I already possess all that was truly intended for me; I am not still "on the way" towards the real thing; fulfilment does not lie in the future for me. No man would ever be capable of saying that, not if he lived to be a hundred and were already standing on the threshold of death.

We have once again used our thematic word. And the question arises: How does it stand with this "not-yet", once the threshold of death has been crossed? At this point we must speak of the information (for the present purely theological) which is comprehended within the idea of termination of the *status viatoris*. What we are told is that man at the moment of death ceases to be "on the way"; dying means finishing the course, ending the "viatoric" state of existence itself. Inner existence, which up to the moment of death possessed not a single element which could be called "final", now attains its irrevocable form. In death the last decision is passed, for good or ill, upon the life as a whole; henceforth nothing in that life can ever again be undone.

Yet we must ask what is the character of this decision. If it represents the uttermost step on the road to self-realization, then it obviously cannot be seen as "coming upon" the man

86

and "descending upon him". Rather, it must be a free act committed from out of the personal centre. Granted, we are compelled to it; the dying person finds himself in a situation in which he cannot do anything but carry out this last decision. But the coercion does not penetrate into the act itself; otherwise there would be no personal act. We shall have occasion to return to this point later.

In the theology of the Church Fathers[8] man's last decision is compared with that of the angel in the first moment of his existence, in which he irrevocably decided for or against God and thus instantly ended the *status viatoris* for himself.[9] This would imply that man at the moment of death "disposes over the whole of existence" in a totally radical and effective way, such as was never possible before for him—the whole, that is, of his own existence. This view is in fact argued by quite a few modern theologians, and with some cogency.[10] It is quite possible, the argument goes, to fall asleep unconsciously, and in fact that is what usually happens; but it is not possible to die unconsciously.[11] On the contrary, it must be assumed that the last decision is absolutely "man's highest act, in which he consummates his existence in freedom".[12] At bottom every ethical decision has this cast, the argument continues, but without achieving full realization; this is why death is not only "an act" but absolutely "*the* act";[13] in a certain sense dying is actually "the only free"[14] and "the first fully personal act of man";[15] thus the most perfect act of earthly life is identical with the act that ends it.[16] So runs this modern theological argument.

Undoubtedly these are bold and at first glance curious ideas. Hearing or reading them, one might for a moment be reminded of Nietzsche's disturbing, overly dithyrambic phrase that a man should "make of his death a festival".[17]

Is not this sort of thing a fanciful attempt to talk away the obvious wretchedness of dying? This question has indeed been asked, and I can well understand it. I think, in fact, that it alerts us to a possible danger. On the other hand I am convinced that the fundamental thesis of there being a final decision which must be made and which is in fact made in dying expresses an indefeasible truth. For we have been explicitly told of something hidden that, in the midst of the terrible event of "natural" dying, nevertheless takes place, perhaps despite all appearances.

But there is some evidence even for this hidden something, and our own inner experience offers further confirmation. Thus, most of us share the feeling that all dying, no matter how much it comes upon us from outside, as a natural event, must be more than a mere cessation of the life functions: that, rather, every human life in truth proceeds to an end and comes to its end and does not merely "cease" at a certain moment. Death, we are saying here, is always an act completing existence from within, a carrying out and conclusion, a real bringing to an end, rounding out of the whole of life, making complete, a signing and sealing. In saying this we are above all voicing the consoling and immediately persuasive idea that strictly speaking there can be no such thing as an untimely or premature death. Rather, a man always dies "at the end of his life", in a far more exact sense than we usually realize. The merit of this idea lies chiefly in the fact that it permits and encourages us not to abandon our conviction that the way of the world is ultimately not a matter of chance, not even here, at this darkest spot. And we at once concur when a French theologian[18] states that this interpretation of death is "worthy in a higher measure" of both man and God because it does away with the dire notion that man is unfairly taken by surprise in his last hour, and has no part in the decision.

"Some die too soon, others too late, few at the right hour" —with these sententious words a leading German literary magazine begins the obituary for its publisher. If we assume that the sentence was not mere rhetoric (although it may well be so), then we must ask: From what earthly standpoint can such a statement be made? On what basis can such a judgment be passed? Of course it is not entirely without meaning to say that death robbed a young man of his future and destroyed the finest hopes others had for him. But naturally this is seeing the matter from outside; what else could it be? His closest friends, who knew the dead man intimately, quite often know differently. And nobody at all knows his real inner history. Jean-Paul Sartre too has asserted that death cannot be in the nature of a "final chord" because chance decides the time of it: "We ought rather to compare ourselves to a man condemned to death who is bravely preparing himself for the ultimate penalty, who is doing everything possible to make a good showing on the scaffold, and who meanwhile is carried off by a flu epidemic."[19] Granted, that is a witty way of putting it, and valid insofar as it makes fun of a desperate effort at seizing control by "preparing for death". Still, this does not describe the true state of affairs. And when Sartre goes on to offer as an example the fate of a young writer with the promise of greatness who suddenly dies "before his time" (Balzac before writing *Les Chouans* would have remained the author of "some execrable novels of intrigue"; and so on)—it is clear that he is considering quite another problem from the one which is under discussion here.[20]

Yet the living language takes account of this way of personal fulfilment and self-realization when it continues undeterred to refer to a good man who died young, perhaps even in childhood, as having attained "early ripeness". And at bottom we all know well that such language is certainly an expression of hope, but not a mere euphemism. Thirty-seven-year-old Helmuth James von Moltke, one of the noblest figures in the German resistance to Nazism, wrote in his magnificent last letter to his wife, the day before his execution: "My life is completed, and I can say of myself: he died old and satiated with life. This does not alter the fact that I would be glad to live a little longer."[21]

To be sure, "termination of the *status viatoris*" is not necessarily and not in every case the same as "fulfilment" even though inner direction towards fulfilment remains a peculiar feature of all dying. The consummation and bringing-to-an end of life in a decision affecting the Whole of existence is indeed present in every man's death—so that to this extent every death is always a real conclusion. Fulfilment, however, means not only decision, but good, correct, saving decision which makes the decider himself complete. Oddly enough, Martin Heidegger in his perceptive remarks on death has not seen this distinction. This failure is connected, I think, with the strange fact that in his *Being and Time,* although he analyses every conceivable aspect of the concept of "ending" (ending as "stopping", as "getting finished", as "disappearing" as "being-at-the-end"),[22] he spends not a single word on the old image of "termination of the *status viatoris*". (This is strange because the phrase must have been familiar to the author from his childhood.) Thus it becomes understandable that Heidegger, while he recognizes every death as a conclusion accomplished in freedom, does not also see that it need not be a fulfilment. "With its death, Dasein [existence] has indeed 'fulfilled its course'. But in doing so, has it necessarily exhausted its specific possibilities? Rather, are not these precisely what get taken away from Dasein? Even unfulfilled Dasein ends. . . . Ending does not necessarily mean fulfilling oneself."

These sentences from *Being and Time* at first sound highly convincing. Nevertheless, the antithesis expressed in them is incomplete and awry; only two possibilities are presented: either purely factual ending and cessation, or fulfilment. But there is a third possibility. This third possibility is that a free decision within the self which puts an end to existence may at the same time be an act of refusal and negation. This, too, is one of the possible ways for historical man to terminate the *status viatoris*.

VI

Death and Freedom

THE time has come to examine several critical doubts which probably have been waiting in the wings. For example, is not this idea of a last decision being performed in the act of dying totally at variance with the ordinary empirical findings? Does it not assume an unaltered command and unimpaired mind which the dying man, according to all we have been able to observe, no longer possesses?

On this point we must repeat something we have already said by implication. We have said that the free act terminating the *status viatoris* takes place at a moment of violently overwhelming crisis, when the forcible rending apart of soul and body is already beginning. It takes place in a breathing spell not yet claimed by the impending catastrophe. The further implication is that the catastrophe itself requires this act of us as a free decision, that we are, as it were, coerced into it over our heads. "Man *must* die his death in freedom; he cannot avoid the death which is imposed upon him as the work of his freedom."[1] "Death provokes freedom"; *la mort provoque la liberté.*[2]

Perhaps it will be objected that this is asserting something even more improbable. But in reality this truly remarkable association of outer coercion and inner freedom involves a recurrent structure which is by no means so alien to our experience, everyone's experience, as it may seem at first glance. It almost seems, as a matter of fact, that death must make us aware of this coercion in order for such freedom to be possible at all. Apparently there is no human experience which possesses more purifying force than the experience of impending death, which is possibly already foreshadowed in extreme pain or in the shock of severe loss. At any rate it is highly significant that people never think of attributing purifying effect to a piece of good fortune. If we think back upon the years of the war, for example, we recognize that we never felt inwardly so "right" and "in order" as at moments of extreme danger; we recall this state of fundamental sense of rightness as one of higher freedom, even though it was imposed upon us purely by external peril. Some such experience is probably behind the notation in Kierkegaard's diary: "In the moment of death a man is helped by the situation to become as true as he can be."[3] This perception is confirmed in the already cited example of young Count Moltke, and in innumerable other testimonies from the scaffolds of the Third Reich. Always, it is precisely the forced confrontation with death which suddenly opens a boundlessly expanding realm of inner freedom. And anyone who reads the notes and letters written in the last hours before execution often senses the wonderment of the victims themselves at this inner experience; in fact, they themselves sometimes remark upon it.

There are quite a few arguments against the death penalty; but the charge cannot be made that it robs a man of his own death. If this could be done at all, it would be more apt to happen in the case of those mortally ill patients (who perhaps pay dearly for this very deception) whose true situation is concealed from them by all the means available to science.[4] Presumably, even these victims of deception cannot be spared the ultimate personal decision; or rather, to put this more precisely, it cannot be withheld from them. Nevertheless, it has been quite rightly said that in comparison to them the criminal condemned to death is in a happy situation.

"Conscious Dying"—under this telling title Harald Poelchau, a German prison chaplain who witnessed many hundreds of executions during the years of tyranny, has recorded his observations.[5] His account, which contains many surprising and moving things, makes two elements especially plain. First, the fierce energy with which a man in this extreme situation seeks to make ultimate order within the space of his interior existence, and the concern, overshadowing all else, to put himself into the fitting state of mind for this last step. "To prepare oneself for death" evidently means just this. Involuntarily we recall the provocative statement that Plato puts into the mouth of Socrates: in fact no one who has not lost his reason fears dying itself; what people fear is something else entirely, going down to Hades laden with injustice.[6] In the face of death, Harald Poelchau attests, it becomes evident that "consciousness of guilt consists not in psychological atavisms or neuroses that psychotherapy might be able to remove, but in recognition of false decisions in life . . . and that such guilt can be removed only by forgiveness, whether this be the forgiveness of God or of men. Unforgiven guilt is the greatest obstacle, particularly in cases of conscious dying, to a man's going to his death with composure and calmness."[7] Perhaps even more important is the additional fact that, of course, none of these condemned men viewed his sentence as anything but an outrageous wrong; but that only those achieved complete peace who had brought themselves to forgive even this wrong.

The second element, described on almost every page of this account, is once again that astonishing sense of freedom arising from the very starkness of the confrontation with death. Anyone who has once set out on the trail of this idea will find it confirmed a hundred times over. Thus, for example, Ernst Jünger in his postwar diaries[8] tells of a memorandum "On the Question of Hostages" which he had to draw up while serving as a German officer during the occupation of France. Years later he reread these papers, which were basically directed against the Nazi policies. They had been preserved by chance. "The reading stirred me for a special reason. I had appended to my report a translation of letters in which the Nantes victims bade farewell to their loved ones immediately before they were to be shot. . . . Now other signs rise up. Now the fear and hatred evaporates; the unclouded picture of the man emerges. The world of murderers, of grim retaliators, of blind masses and blind governors subsides into darkness; a great light casts its glow ahead." So here is still another body of evidence given us by an observer, to the effect that the massive oppression and violence ultimately drives the hunted and harried man to enter, at the very last moment in which the irrevocable gravity of the situation is upon him, into an area of existence unconfined by coercion, a broad open space, as it were, which suddenly also permits "time enough" for him to carry out that total disposition of his now concluded present existence. This of course does not mean that the ultimate inner order is attained in every case, or that it comes of its own accord; the decision may take quite another turn. Nevertheless, the fact remains that the extreme situation at least poses the challenge and thus lets the individual take in full freedom the last step on his course. And by his so doing the whole journey once and for all receives its meaning.

Whoever would gloss over either of these two elements in

mortality—the being overpowered and the freedom—is dealing falsely with the situation. Sartre[9] is quite right when he takes issue with the "freedom towards death" which Heidegger claims as "my peculiar possibility". Sartre objects that dying, no less than being born, is an objective process "which as such on principle escapes me". We can also understand Sartre's thesis that death is meaningless and absurd if it is nothing more than mere external fact, *un pur fait*; if, in other words, it "does not appear on the foundation of our freedom".[10] However, Sartre himself explicitly denies this freedom aspect of dying, and thus is cut off from insight into the full reality of death.

Theologians, too, sometimes speak as if we are faced with the alternative of understanding death either as an external, almost juridical decree of God, which man can only endure passively, or else as "the phenomenon of personal existence's having reached its term."[11] Such an either-or misses the crucial point. Even the inexorable biblical dictum about the tree which, once fallen, lies where it fell (Ecc. 11.3) actually contains both aspects, although it seems to speak of nothing but blind chance and dark nemesis. On the one hand the falling itself, as well as the time of falling, is decreed and not within the power of man; but on the other hand the direction of the fall is open, can be corrected up to the last moment, and is left to the freedom of man.

Whoever accepts the idea—with Socrates and Plato and the whole humane tradition—of a judgment after death, and consequently perceives man's death as an event which brings in its train and makes possible an infallible, irrevocable verdict upon the life which has now reached its end, takes it for granted that this judgment must be preceded by and based on the final free decision, affecting the whole of life, of the individual being judged. That judgment is based, that is, on an act in which the man "chooses for eternity the attitude which he desires in truth".[12] That act may, of course, be nothing more than affirmation of the life he has lived up to that moment.

But is it not extremely improbable that the dying person in the ordinary case will be capable at all of such a freely disposing act of decision? After all, the man condemned to death is not yet a dying man. He confronts what awaits him with the unclouded mental powers of the healthy person and obviously is in a totally different condition from, say, someone fatally injured in a traffic accident. Similarly, the situation of one who after long illness gradually loses consciousness and fades out of existence is again entirely different.

In answer to these points I would suggest, first of all, that the condemned man is not differently situated from the dying man; perhaps for him the fate of death is even incomparably nearer and surer than for the ordinary dying man. On the other hand, the special nature of his circumstances brings out more forcibly, hammers out, we might say, that paradoxical structure of violence associated with freedom which is peculiar to all human death. The circumstances bring this out more clearly than in the normal case of natural, that is not-imposed death, in which the finality of the moment, the *terminus ad quem*, remains obscured and equivocal, so that up to the last it can always be imagined that "it isn't serious yet". In this respect, then, non-violent, "natural" dying is as it were not a "pure case"—strangely enough, we might add, unless we have given ourselves a timely reminder that the absolutely paradigmatic death was the death of a condemned man.

How then, once more, can there be free disposition over

one's own existence as a whole if death or unconsciousness may ensue from one moment to the next—in an accidental explosion, in an air raid, in a plane crash, in a cerebral haemorrhage? I reply with a counter-question: How many units of measurable time do we need for a decision? Are we not able, for example, to dream in a fraction of a second of an event which stretches over years? Perhaps it may be said that this sort of thing happens only in dreams. But that is no argument. What is manifest in dreams is that our psyche, our soul, can set aside temporal successiveness to a great extent, and that, as the old writers expressed it, the power of the mind is itself something above and beyond time, *supra tempus.*[13] We know also, on the basis of immediate experience, that for the performance of an act of loving concern (for example) no more than an instant is needed, an infinitesimally small span of time which no one will ever be able to measure with a chronometer. Again and again we hear it reported that people who have been rescued from the imminent threat of death have at the moment before losing consciousness seen their entire life, with all the details thought to be long since forgotten, or actually forgotten, unrolling with perfect clarity before their mind's eye.[14] If man has this faculty, surely it represents an opportunity, an invitation and with it an endowment, for a comprehensive estimate and judgment, perhaps for a condemnation, of the dying person's own life, on the basis of the highest imaginable, absolute standard. Precisely this, then, would be that last step on the path of man's inner existence, the step by which and in which the individual attains his last unalterable shape and form, the one he himself ultimately wants and affirms.

To be sure, the "act" in which this happens may well be an unnoticeable sigh, heard by no one, a sound that, perhaps, the dying person himself can no longer articulate, perhaps even—because, like ecstatic contemplation, it demands the full, undiminished energies of the soul[15]—even beyond the reach of his own reflecting consciousness.

This last statement has been made with something of a side glance at weighty objections which spring to mind at once. Do not loss of consciousness, helplessness, inability to communicate, anaesthesia, and so on, exclude the act we have been discussing?

From time immemorial mankind's fundamental convictions have answered this question with a categorical No. "All secular doctrines of death in all ages and among all peoples must be understood in terms of man's profound desire to transmute death into an act of his own freedom."[16] Christendom, moreover, has never failed to consider a dying person a *subjectum capax* for the sacraments even when he no longer presents any signs of conscious life, or may seem already deceased. That is, he is treated as someone who can and is willing to receive the salvation the sacramental symbols are meant to bestow. Of course the proponents of positivistic enlightenment have always considered this practice as obscurantist magic and dismissed it as prescientific naïveté, a piece of atavistic primitivism. But it is surprising to have that old conviction confirmed by certain findings brought to light in the past few decades by empirical investigation of man in general and death in particular. These findings have at any rate confirmed rather than refuted the old assumptions. It has long been known that clarity of consciousness and even distinct perception of the environment can coexist with total incapacity to communicate. But aside from that, psychosomatic medicine and psychoanalytic studies have

99

shown that the vital decisions affecting the fate of the individual are made largely in a zone of our beings which is inaccessible to the probings of consciousness. And if modern "thanatology", operating with the precise methods of measurement and description available to scientific physiology and pathology, has grasped anything at all, it has learned the difficulty of determining what really happens in human death. First and foremost, precisely because of new techniques of artificial reanimation and prolongation of life, death turns out to be a process of infinite stages taking place gradually over an unexpectedly long period of time. It is by no means concluded with what is commonly called "death", meaning "relative" or "clinical" death.[17]

Naturally, none of this proves unequivocally that an act of free decision does indeed conclude earthly life. But those who hold otherwise cannot very well appeal to scientific arguments. In reality the matter is of a sort that by its nature cannot be checked. After all, every human decision takes place in a cell accessible only to the actor. How much more is this true for the last decision, the essence of which is, to use a phrase of Karl Rahner's,[18] that the actor together with his act vanishes from even his own field of vision.

That "last step" on the way can, incidentally, be taken only at the end of life; that is of the essence of the matter. One can prepare oneself for it, but preparation does not fix the moment or quality of the step. The conditions under which it must be taken are absolutely new, have never existed before, and are not comparable to any previous situation of decision. To put it briefly, this last decision can in no way be anticipated; it is on principle not foreseeable.

That fact has its bearing on what "learning to die" might consist of, assuming that something of the sort exists. What

the "purely" philosophical doctrines of death have to say
about this matter, explicitly or implicitly, seems exceedingly
non-pertinent, practically useless and actually hopeless—
especially when, for example, it is suggested that we make
it a point of honour not to submit, rather defy death by
ourselves "choosing" the inevitable. We have already discussed briefly this fairly ancient recommendation which
constantly reappears in new variants. But the profound dis-
cord and hidden infirmity, with which the Stoic doctrine
was already infected at its root in classical times, is nowhere
revealed so baldly as in its attitude towards death. There is
nothing surprising about this. The maxim not to let our
hearts be affected and shaken by anything may on occasion
be quite worthy of respect; but it must become absurd in the
face of an event whose whole importance consists in shaking
to the very depths not only the energies of our soul, but our
existence itself. Thus it is rather dubious advice that Michel
de Montaigne offers us in the chapter we have already cited
once before, "That to philosophize is to learn to die": "And
to begin to strip it [death] of its greatest advantage against
us, let us take an entirely different way from the usual one.
Let us rid it of its strangeness, come to know it, get used to
it. Let us have nothing on our minds as often as death. At
every moment let us picture it in our imagination in all its
aspects. At the stumbling of a horse, the fall of a tile, the
slightest pinprick, let us promptly chew on this: Well, what
if it were death itself? And thereupon let us tense ourselves
and make an effort."[19]

As a general rule, so-called "thinking about death" is
probably a poor way of learning to die. Georges Bernanos in
one of his last imaginative works, the *Dialogues des Carmélites*, has the dying prioress say: "I have meditated on

death every hour of my life, but that does not help me at all now."[20] And when the philosopher Peter Wust learned for certain that he would never leave his sickbed, he asked in a diary note, evidently with profound surprise, why all philosophy failed him now.

It would seem that the only meaningful preparation for death, true learning to die, would have to consist in somehow "practising" or "getting used to"—perhaps without especially thinking about death or even talking about it—that never foreseeable last free decision which will be required of a man when he dies. But what is the nature of this decision?

We have so far described it, in a somewhat neutral phrase, as a person's having total disposition over himself. But what precisely is disposed? What must the nature of this disposition be if it is actually to bring the course of this present physical life to the end it intends for itself? The most convincing answer to this question runs as follows: <u>Man's final disposition, his last will and testament as it were,</u> with which he simultaneously concludes and completes his earthly existence, <u>is a religious act of loving devotion</u>[21] <u>in which the individual, explicitly accepting death as his destiny, offers up himself, and the life now slipping from him, to God</u>. Naturally that is no philosophical answer. It is the answer of Christian theology—although, incidentally, there is far more to it than that.[22] But to the philosophically-minded person who accords it some thought, this answer is convincing, as I have said, because it coincides with the experience of lived existence. For what this experience unswervingly suggests as the hidden structure of all life lived in a truly meaningful way is something the individual—even if he affirms this structural law—is never compelled to take with absolute seriousness, and indeed can never do so throughout his lifetime: namely, that one possesses only what one lets go of, and that one loses what one tries to hold. What is required of man in the moment of death, for the first and only time, is to realize this very thing. It is required, but at that moment he is also enabled to do so; he is expected literally, not just "by intention", not just "in good will", not just symbolically and rhetorically, but in reality to lose his life in order to gain it.[23]

But here a new question promptly arises: to gain *what* life?

VII

Immortality—of what?

THE magnificent passage from Jean-Paul Sartre, part of which we have already quoted, that our life is made up "not only of waitings, but of waitings which themselves wait for waitings", ends with a surprisingly sinister conclusion. At first Sartre proceeds with the same keenness: "These waitings evidently all include a reference to a final term (*un terme ultime*) which would be *waited for* without waiting for anything more. A repose which would be *being* and no longer a waiting for being. The whole series is suspended from this final term." All this is clear, and precisely and persuasively formulated. But now he continues: "Christians have tried to take death as this final term," *de donner la mort comme ce terme ultime.*[1] This is, it seems to me, a curious distortion of the image of the termination of the *status viatoris*.

Dying certainly means: finishing the way, as well as finishing the "being-on-the-way"; it means "completing the course". But it flouts the plain meaning of such language to say or mean that the decisive fact is that the course is no longer being run, that one has come to a stop, that the pilgrimage and the forward movement simply ceases—as if the waiting embodied in this viatoric existence were formally directed towards the mere termination of our roaming rather than towards reaching our goal, towards arrival, towards achieving and receiving the thing for whose sake and towards which we have been on our way. In other words, the waitings of which human life is truly composed are not directed towards death itself, and not towards being dead. No one who really understands dying as termination of the *status viatoris* can ever have held such an opinion. Anyone who has taken a road to the end has not merely put something behind him; at the same time something new begins. Behind that idea has always lain the assumption that man's waitings, or more exactly, his hope, is directed towards something. To be sure, he can gain it only in dying, but it lies beyond death and therefore still exists beyond it. Above all, inherent in the thought, whether we realize it or not, is the idea that there is something in man himself that arrives somewhere after termination of the course and that therefore persists undestroyed through the event of death and in spite of it.

Although to be sure "termination of the *status viatoris*" means "end" in a most emphatic sense (so that, as we have already said, that "end" seems almost a more final affair than the separation of body and soul)—there is nevertheless an element in the concept that proclaims itself "non-end", that insists on transition, future, continuance, even new beginning. In other words, *within* the description of death itself there inevitably arises the question of indestructibility and imperishability of the soul, no matter how conceived; the question, that is, of what is ordinarily and not very felicitously called its "immortality".

For some time there has been a rather involved controversy centring around this concept. The individual voices are difficult to distinguish, nor is it easy to make out the opposing positions ascribed to them. The clearest is the old argument of metaphysical materialism, which regards man as a part of the material cosmos. Consequently, for the proponents of this view the problem of "personal" continuance after death does not exist at all. Death simply "abolishes" man as an individual; all that happens is a return to the total material process of the universe. In a word, when the individual dies he is extinguished, body and soul. Astonishingly, there is a school within modern Protestant theology which, starting though it does from entirely different premises, in fact advocates the same thesis: "Human dying is a true 'being-at-an end' and no hidden 'continuance' and 'life after death'";[2] "the Christian religion recognizes no immortality".[3] Its most radical formulation has already been cited here: "The New Testament teaches that not only the body but also the soul dies."[4] The considerations underlying these bold statements have likewise been expressed clearly. There are two principal ones. First, it is held that the reality of death is attenuated if there were to be anything in us that is *not* mortal. And, secondly, once death ceases to be regarded as real, belief in the Resurrection is negated.[5] So runs the argument. Either immortality of the soul or Resurrection of the dead; both cannot be true together. "Resurrection: that is the grave burst open. . . . Immortality: that is the grave denied."[6]

If we look for the adversary against whom these challenging phrases are being hurled, we meet a new complication. Three principal counter-positions are mentioned: the Enlightenment's idealistic doctrine of immortality; Greek metaphysics; traditional Catholic theology. Of the last, it is held, by the way, that ". . . at this point it . . . stands under the influence of Greek philosophy",[7] on the one hand, and that on the other hand there is "no very great difference between the Enlightenment's idea of immortality and that of the Middle Ages".[8] The latter term refers primarily to the great scholastics, who with considerable justice are regarded as more or less the spokesmen of Catholic doctrinal tradition.

The above is a highly summary sketch of the present state of the dispute over "immortality". As might be expected, it reflects not only the complexity of the subject itself, but also the involved interplay of influences and polemics within the whole history of thought. For example, the conception of "Greek" philosophy, which is held to be incompatible with the biblical doctrine of man, is largely the product of an extremely dubious "interpretation" of Plato. And as for the incomparably more difficult case of Catholic theology, there are of course rationalistic, idealistic, evolutionistic and other influences and theses represented in it, just as there are in Protestant theology. On the other hand, the veritable *thesaurus* of traditional materials contained within Catholic theology could scarcely be translated into a system of explicit theses. One modern Catholic theologian[9] has recently said, for example, that anyone searching for biblical testimonies to immortality "would have to cite the entire New Testament", whereas another[10] has concurrently commented: "He who speaks of 'immortality' . . . where the Bible talks of men's being dead . . . is unprepared for what the Fathers of the Church have lauded as the grace of *athanasia*." We may say that those who cannot grasp the common denominator of these two statements, which are equally justified by the tradition, will never comprehend the doctrine of immortality contained in the theology underlying them.

Nevertheless, we repeat, we still do not intend to engage in denominational apologetics or controversial theology, nor in any theology at all. On the other hand there is little profit in ignoring the presence of all the above-mentioned participants in the discussion—and in fact the philosopher must not ignore them. On the contrary, our examination of the problem—even though as a philosophical investigation it must base itself primarily on the reality encountered—naturally and definitely takes place within the framework of the discussion as it already exists. Greek philosophy, idealism, materialism, Enlightenment, and the whole range of variations in Christian interpretation of Christian doctrine—all this taken together, and perhaps several other aspects, provides the historical standpoint from which to proceed to a concrete position on the subject, cast in the form of question and answer, or even of challenge. We simply cannot sidestep this confrontation in the pursuit of an argument, however "purely philosophical" we intend to keep it. If we try to sidestep it, we find ourselves without any standpoint at all, floating in a void without reverberation or structure. Should anyone think otherwise, I can only recommend that he try, as I have done, to discuss the subject of "death and immortality" at universities in India.

It would seem that the crux of the present controversy is still that repudiation of the traditional concept of immortality which first appeared in the philosophical and literary works of the decades before and after the French Revolution. Its effect on contemporaries must have been of a violence we can scarcely comprehend nowadays.

In the year 1767 one of the most influential books of German Enlightenment philosophy was published: Moses Mendelssohn's *Phaedo, or on the Immortality of the Soul.* Hermann Hettner, in his *History of German Literature in the Eighteenth Century*, has remarked that for the public of the period this book was "not just a philosophical treatise, but a powerful religious piece of education and consolation"; "from all sides" people "turned to him, the Jew, for advice and pastoral care".[11] In 1780, a year before his death, Lessing in his *Education of the Human Race* summed up the entire doctrine of Christianity in a single sentence: "And so Christ became the first reliable practical teacher of the immortality of the soul."[12] In 1794 in France Robespierre, disciple of Rousseau, had the Convention promulgate the famous decree, a single paragraph in length, stating that the French nation believed in the immortality of the soul as well as in a Supreme Being. Then there is the story of Goethe's outburst in a conversation with Eckermann (February 25, 1824). Leafing through an album, Goethe came upon something by the popular poet Christoph August Tiedge, and began talking about him and the poem *Urania*, a "best seller" published in 1801. Although, as Eckermann remarks, Goethe was at the time in the most genial of moods, he suddenly and passionately recalled the years in which he had "endured a good deal" on account of this book. *Urania* is a didactic poem of six cantos which casts into verse the Kantian doctrine of immortality. It is by now absolutely unreadable. Nevertheless, it is worth noting the final stanza of this poem, in which, incidentally, Immortality is introduced and addressed as an allegorical person:

> "When my eyes their final tears have shed
> You beckon, call me to divinity.
> A *man*, a pilgrim, lays down his weary head,
> A *god* begins his passage instantly."

Goethe spoke of the time "when nothing was sung and nothing declaimed except *Urania*. Wherever you went, you found the *Urania* on all tables; *Urania* and immortality were the subject of every conversation." And he complained that "stupid women who plumed themselves on believing in immortality along with Tiedge" had sometimes "examined

[him] on this point in a very conceited way".

And so on. Countless other references might be cited to show that the idea of immortality seems to have been "the real central dogma of the Enlightenment"[13] as well as, it has been said, "the last vestige of personal piety still left over from historical Christianity" in this period.[14]

On the other hand, the connection with Christian dogmatic tradition is extremely dubious. For what was there really to all those notions of immortality which everyone discussed so passionately? Back of it all was the "great lie"[15] —that (first) death is something fundamentally unreal, a mere transition which scarcely affects the core of our being, and that (secondly) life on the other side of death is nothing but a "continuance" of life here, except for being "virtuous" and sustained by the individual's own spiritual powers. Thus, in Kant's words, "what we call the immortality of the soul is the existence and personality, continuing into infinity, of the same rational being".[16] This is a "better", a blissful existence, of course, in that the soul "is exalted from an imperfect, sensual life to a perfect, everlasting, spiritual life",[17] in which the limitations and indigence of physical life are finally overcome—man, after all, is an "indigent being" only "to the extent that he belongs to the world of sense". This last phrase likewise comes from *Kant's Critique of Practical Reason*.[18]

I have deliberately chosen to cite the distinctive language of the great German systematic philosophers. Quotation serves as a kind of touchstone, for we realize suddenly how utterly remote many of their fundamental ideas have already become to us. Fichte,[19] for example, apostrophizes the imperishability of the human mind in the following terms— not in a poem, *nota bene*, but in his lectures on the destiny of the scholar: "What is called death cannot interrupt my work . . . I have . . . seized hold of eternity. I lift my head boldly to the threatening precipice, to the raging cataract and to the rumbling clouds swimming in a sea of fire, and say: I am eternal, and I defy your power. Rend apart the last mote of the body I call mine: my will alone . . . will soar boldly and coldly above the ruins of the universe."

Such a style of thinking and talking has, as everyone realizes, altogether disappeared from our midst, and what has followed the idealistic *philosophie rose* is unmistakably a *philosophie noire*—although the question remains whether the existentialist philosophy of absurdity (for example) may not be merely an aching, desperate form of the same idealistic absolutizing of autonomous man. We shall have a word more to say about that later.

First of all, it seems quite understandable that after such inordinate misuse there should arise an overwhelming desire not even to mention the word "immortality" for a century at least. Understandable, above all, is the protest of Christian theologians that "immortality" has nothing whatsoever to do with the doctrines of the New Testament. And we can heartily agree with Simone Weil when she calls belief in immortality "harmful" because it "robs death of its purpose".[20]

Nevertheless, immortality is one of the fundamental words in all language. And fundamental words cannot be annihilated by decree. How often do we not wish we could eliminate the word "love" from the vocabulary, because it too seems to have been totally worn out and empty. But this word, exactly like the word "immortality", is irreplaceable; we cannot do without it.[21] What we can do and must do is this: by ever alert, ever repeated efforts to attempt to keep the true, original meaning of the words flawlessly before our minds.

At this point, however, certain theologians might protest that the idea of the spiritual soul's being endowed with imperishability by virtue of which it is ultimately unaffected by death and simply continues to exist in a "better" life—this idea is nothing but the doctrine of the great Greeks, Plato above all; hence it is at any rate a specifically *philosophical* doctrine, the product of a purely rational view of the world and man and *for that very reason* not significant to the Christian, unacceptable by him, and above all not to be reconciled with the New Testament![22] The trouble with Enlightenment theology, and incidentally with medieval scholasticism, of course, thus consists (the argument continues) not in any "*mis*use" of the concept of immortality but in the very *use* of this philosophical (metaphysical, Greek, pagan) category and the efforts to make it coincide with Christian doctrine.

This is, patently, a clear and far-reaching position. Strictly speaking, two different points are involved. The first concerns the fundamental incompatibility of any philosophical anthropology, and philosophy in general, with Christian theology and the New Testament. The whole burden of this book, and not this book alone, has from the start been aimed at refuting and correcting this view, as will shortly emerge. The second point holds that Enlightenment theology essentially took over and reproduced Plato's special doctrine of immortality. To be sure, the theologians of the Enlightenment repeatedly claimed they had done so, and perhaps sincerely believed they had, but we mean to show that the contrary is rather the case. We must now discuss this matter briefly. Plato, after all, is not just anybody, but one of the founders of all European thinking about man, and still capable of setting the tone of philosophical discussion. Moreover, rationalistic distortions of Plato have had tremendous influence by way of popular philosophy, literature and many other channels, and continue to wield influence down to the present day.

Moses Mendelssohn's *Phaedo* is a rather curious book. In large part it is simply a translation of the Platonic dialogue *Phaedo*. But the boundary where the translator becomes an author in his own right is not clearly marked. The preface states that an attempt is being made "to arrange the metaphysical proofs according to the taste of our times", and that towards the end the editor felt himself obliged "to abandon" his guide, that is, Plato.[23] But Mendelssohn's work too, focused from start to finish on the conversation between Socrates and his friends held in the death cell on the day before the execution. And the innocent reader accepted the whole as a somewhat "modernized" but nevertheless genuine Plato, in other words as a contemporary interpretation of Plato.

All very well, one might say, what objection could there be to that? Such editings are customary nowadays, too; after all, Mendelssohn did not turn the *Phaedo* into a television serial![23a] Of course that is true; but the decisive question remains whether the interpretation was *valid*. If we place the two texts side by side. Mendelssohn's and Plato's *Phaedo*, and compare them, it soon develops that we have two utterly different books before us, and that Mendelssohn's modernization suppresses and distorts the very heart of Plato's argument to the point of unrecognizability.

For example, the reader of Mendelssohn would not know

that Plato's work contains no rational speculation at all about
what may come after death. Rather, all that is said about the
world beyond in the Platonic dialogues, not only in the
Phaedo, is explicitly credited to "myth", that is to say, to a
source other than Plato, one which he respects and venerates
as the "sacred tradition". "I must use a pagan to avoid
becoming involved with Revelation"[24]—thus Mendelssohn
wrote to a friend while he was working on the book, without
appreciating what it meant that Plato, for his part, emphatically "became involved" in the truth of mythic accounts of
judgment after death and the fate of the dead in the beyond
—accounts which he himself never would have claimed to
have invented. In the eighteenth-century *Phaedo* there is in
fact not a word to be found concerning this eschatological
myth; Mendelssohn simply deleted it. Not only is this a
crucial omission, but it falsifies what remains; the instrumen-
tation of the whole no longer harmonizes.

Furthermore, it would never occur to one, after reading
Mendelssohn's *Phaedo*, that according to Plato, "this" world
and the "other" world are separated not only by death, but
by the Judgment; and that no form of existence in the beyond
is conceivable which would not be a disposition granted after
divine judgment. According to Plato, that is, life beyond
death as an object of human hope could certainly not be
mere continued existence of the soul. Socrates says it clearly;
for one who does not desire the good, immortality is a terrible
danger[25]—because "those who are thought to be incurable
because of the greatness of their crimes" are hurled into
Tartarus "whence they never come out".[26] Karl Barth, evidently under the sway of the rationalistic falsification of
Plato on this point, in a radio lecture[27] on the subject of immortality spoke of the man opposed to God as being lost and

subject to eternal death—and appended the remark: "Plato did not put it this way." But the truth is that Plato put "it" exactly this way. In Plato's opinion "true bliss" exists for the good not, as Mendelssohn makes his enlightened hero say, "in the beauties and perfections of my mind",[28] but (at any rate, so we may read in *Phaedo*) in dwelling in that place where the temples house not the images of the gods, but the gods themselves.[29]

These few random remarks are, then, intended to clear away some fundamental errors introduced by the Enlightenment's interpretation of Plato, and prevalent ever since. Certain long-standing misconceptions of the Platonic doctrine of death and immortality must be cleared away. First, it can no longer be said that for Plato the survival of the soul consists in a mere continued existence, the soul by virtue of its natural potency moving on into the infinite. Second, the theory that the "Greek" doctrine of immortality is a "purely philosophical" doctrine in the sense that it is founded exclusively on empirical evidence and rational argumentation can no longer be maintained. Plato, at any rate, clearly did not see it that way. And finally, this puts an end to the notion that the "Greek" conception of what happens to the human soul on the other side of death is totally at variance with the Christian conception. Even so, we might very well agree with Oscar Cullmann that "Paul surely . . . must have met people who could not accept his preaching of the Resurrection precisely because they believed in the immortality of the soul".[30]

In regard, incidentally, to the Platonic use of this phrase, "immortality of the soul", one more emendation is in order. In our simplistic approach to the whole question, we have fallen into the habit of taking this phrase to stand for the basic Platonic concept, of considering that the soul, which must also be understood as the "real man", is the part of man which is immortal. But probably this is standard only to "Platonism". Plato himself, however, is no Platonist. At any rate, in the late dialogue *Phaedrus*, when he launches on what seems a wholly fresh approach to the question of "in what sense a living being is termed mortal or immortal", he suddenly ceases to speak of the soul alone. "We think," he says, "of a living being, spiritual and physical at once, but both, soul and body, united for all time."[31] Moreover, he goes on, immortality is not to be regarded as a mere rational concept susceptible to demonstration; rather, we think of it with our minds on "the god whom we have never seen, nor fully conceived".

Though he is chary of venturing on a definition, Plato seems to be suggesting: If ever immortality is conferred upon us, not just the soul but the entire physical human being will in some inconceivable manner participate in the life of the gods; for in them alone is it made real in its original perfection. "Among the Greeks, he who says 'immortal' says God."[32] Plato himself, therefore, here concedes that it is a catachrestic, inadequate, use of language to call the soul immortal.

Nevertheless, it is not without significance that this word repeatedly makes its way into Plato's text, and into everyone's living language and comes to mind whenever the subject is touched on—even though, strictly speaking, one should speak only of the *indestructibility* of the soul. For what is in truth forever meant by this indestructibility is the immortality, exceeding all conception—not of the soul, but of the whole man.

VIII

Indestructibility and Eternal Life

THE established phrase "immortality of the soul" is mis-
leading, inasmuch as, strictly speaking, only the man but not
the soul can die or not die. What is more, the mere word
promotes the misconception that at bottom the man does
not "really" die at all. Hence it would be better to speak of ✓
the indestructibility of the soul, or its imperishability—as
the great teachers of Christendom in fact always do. These
terms also evoke the destructive violence of death; merely to
use them is to emphasize that violence—even as they assert ·
that the soul does not entirely succumb to this destruction.
"The man who has died is dead, although his soul lives"—
Hermann Volk[1] admits that this may sound like an absurdity; but after all, he adds, man altogether, even the living
man, is "a reality hard to comprehend".

Nevertheless, we must try to see what is meant by that
ultimate and extreme invulnerability, or whatever we choose
to call it. On so important a matter we have, I should think, a
right to the most exact information it is possible to obtain.
And we shall not be put off by such facile vague phrases as,
surprisingly enough, even a Karl Jaspers[2] offers: "The
presence of the Eternal is in itself immortality"; "we are
mortal where we are loveless, immortal where we love".
That is far too blurred a statement. What, then, is exactly
meant by "imperishability of the soul"?

"That is perishable which possibly cannot be; that is
imperishable, *incorruptibile*, which cannot possibly not be."

Thus Thomas Aquinas in his commentary on Aristotle's *Metaphysics*.[3] This, certainly, is a clear enough statement. But can the human soul really be called imperishable in such a sense? Is not some even more stringent definition or perhaps reservation needed? Are not these terms too literal and "absolute" to be applied to the human soul? And did Aquinas mean them to be? When, for example, we read in Spinoza's *Ethics*: "Our mind is eternal," *mens nostra aeterna est*,[4] and when Goethe calls the mind "a being . . . of entirely indestructible nature" and "a continuing force from eternity to eternity"[5]—both are saying that the soul is "imperishable", that by definition it is of such a nature that it cannot possibly not be. Nevertheless, it is quite clear that Thomas Aquinas would passionately reject any such mode of thinking and speaking. Yet from the language of his definition, he is defenceless against such an interpretation. It can indeed be confounded with his own, which is to say with the traditional Western concept of the imperishability of the soul. This equating of the two different views is no abstract possibility; one finds this out as soon as one begins to participate in the contemporary controversy on our subject.

Differentiation from still another angle appears to be even more difficult. Arthur Schopenhauer expressed that other viewpoint as follows: "The most solid ground for our imperishability is, after all, the old proposition that nothing real can ever revert to nothingness, *in nihilum nihil potest reverti*."[6] "In spite of millennia of death and decay nothing has as yet been lost, not an atom of matter, still less anything of the inner being which presents itself as Nature. Accordingly we can with good cheer cry out at any moment: 'In spite of time, death and decay we are all still here.'"[7] One need not go to great lengths to point out that this rather desperate-sounding encouragement says not a word about the specific indestructibility of the spiritual soul. On the other hand, the soul too, of course, would have to partake in such universal stability of being, if such really exists. And Thomas Aquinas too, in formulating the traditional doctrine of Christendom, seems to maintain exactly that; at any rate he says something which at first reading sounds confoundingly similar: "No created being can be called absolutely perishable";[8] "all works of God persist in Eternity".[9] At a second reading, however, the fundamental difference can be discerned: Thomas is speaking of the universe as *Creation*. That changes the matter, and complicates it as well.

One who considers the universe, as well as body-and-soul man himself, as *creatura,* as having proceeded from the absolute, existence-determining will of the *Creator* and thus having received its being from this creative source—one who takes this view cannot possibly regard such existence, summoned forth from the void, as so inherently stable that there can be no thought of its reversion to nothingness. A creature is by definition incapable of maintaining itself in being by its own powers. To be sure, we likewise cannot take the step into nothingness by our own powers, no matter how much we may long to do so. In fact we are, in a sense that must be taken very literally, "*incapable* of not being". Nevertheless, the fact remains: "Created beings could return to nothingness as they emerged from it—provided that pleased God."[10] For no one but the Creator could revoke and undo the act of creating.[11] In view of the infinite debasement of Creation by historical man, that undoing might even be an act of *justice*—such a thought is not altogether alien to the Christian tradition.[12]

But all that is only the negative side of the coin, so to speak. The other side is shown in the sentence: "God 'has created all things that they might be' [Wisdom 1:14] and not that they might revert to nothingness."[13] This means: the single ultimate guarantee of the stability of being is the unchangeable will of the Creator, by virtue of which all reality not only exists but also is "good" in itself, that is, creatively affirmed and loved. And in fact one who believes in the creatureliness of the universe and of himself, finds in the concept "real" itself, *eo ipso*, an incomparable "positiveness" and an immutable continuance such as the positivist with his vaunted respect for sheer facticity has not the slightest inkling of. Perhaps he may not realize this until he finds himself in an extreme intellectual or existential situation. At a Chinese Buddhist monastery, for example, my hosts once set out, though only half seriously, to give me a practical demonstration of the principles of Zen meditation by repeating to me dozens of times that I was in reality "nothing" and "no one". At last I could discover no way to defend myself against the uncanny suction and beguilement of this "nihilation" except by proclaiming aloud: No, I am both a "something" and a "somebody"— because God has created me.

In creation something happens that absolutely cannot be undone again; the creature which has once entered existence can never again vanish totally from reality. This indestructibility of the soul inherent in creatureliness alone rules out the idea that after death everything can once again be exactly as it was before. Surprisingly, Karl Barth,[14] discussing the "testimony of the Bible", once said that to be mortal means for man the equivalent of existing "within not outside the temporal term set for him; as he was not before, so he is not afterwards". I ask myself whether that can really be asserted if "before" means: before his creation.

We are still endeavouring to come to a closer definition of the concept of "imperishability of the soul", and we still have not spoken formally of the specific imperishability which distinguishes the spiritual soul. I do not mean merely that it cannot be lost, however this may be conceived, or that it remains within the framework of Creation as a whole.[15] I mean that it is in some way inviolable, so that it can persist ✓ and be preserved in being beyond death in its very own individuality. Nevertheless, we have already had our accounting with the idealistic proposition that man's mind possesses its life out of its own substance and maintains itself in existence out of its own powers "continuing in force from eternity to eternity". Incidentally, the nihilistic philosophy of absurdity, though it speaks almost exclusively of death and frustration, is despite all appearances determined at its root by the very same claim of human godlikeness. We have already called this the aching and desperate form of the idealistic doctrine of autonomous man. One might also say that the difference consists in this: that existentialism advances the same claim in the *modus* of disappointment. To be disappointed means not finding the world as it "really" should be according to one's lights. But one who knows himself to be no more and no less than what he truly is—*creatura*, a creature of God—cannot be disappointed that he is not "like God".

He also will not view the specific imperishability of the soul—although by that is meant a stability which cannot be affected either by intervention from outside or by any impairment of his own capability of being—he will not view this *incorruptibilitas* as though it were a sovereign potency which bursts the bounds of creatureliness. The individual imperishability of the soul is, of course, likewise something received when the individual was created. That means that it is something given to us as really our own, which is henceforth a permanent part of our beings.

In saying this I am prepared for a certain theological objection, one long associated with the disputation into which I have plunged and which I neither can nor wish to evade. The objection was raised long ago; Leibniz, for example, was among those who attempted to answer it. Are we not claiming for man, it is argued,[16] an "absolute" immortality which in truth does not belong to him—"absolute" in the sense that it has its root in the nature of the soul rather than the will of God? Leibniz[17] replied that for the cause of religion it is "much more valuable, *infiniment plus avantageux*, to show that souls are by nature immortal, and that, were they not, it would be a miracle, than to assert that our souls by nature must die and do not die solely thanks to a miraculous grace dependent on a divine promise." Probably the mistrust which sparks this particular objection is not removed, rather intensified, by this answer. The decisive factor, I would say, is what we mean by creation and creating. If *creatio* means that God, in creating, does not retain Being for himself so that he still remains the *Sole* reality, but truly gives and shares it, then obviously the *creatura* possesses existence and essence as vertitable property, received as always from God, the ceaselessly effective Source of everything, but for this very reason real property. Everything that man is and possesses "by virtue of Creation" he is and possesses "by nature". I would therefore reply to the objection with a countering question: Does not our natural endowment of being, including the individual imperishability of the soul, have its foundation likewise in "the will of God"?

But if *incorruptibilitas* really appertains by nature to the spiritual soul—should not this quality also be perceptible and verifiable by the thinking mind, no less perceptible, at any rate, than the soul itself? That, precisely, is what we are asserting here! The indestructibility of the spiritual soul is not a matter that can be merely divined, conjectured or believed; it can be demonstrated and made convincing by arguments. It ought to be clear, however, what sort of arguments can be expected in this case, and what sort cannot.

Obviously we are not in the realm of direct empirical evidence—and so there cannot be any simple "proof from experience". Still less are we in the transparent area of quantitativeness—which means that we can achieve nothing by measurements and calculations. As for the sciences not concerned primarily with quantitative procedures, the biologist Adolf Portmann stated some time ago "that no one will obtain from natural science in its present state a scientific explanation of the origin and destiny of living organisms; that applies no less to a flower or a bird than to a man."[18] In other words, biology "is not competent to answer the question of immortality";[19] it cannot legitimately investigate the subject at all. What all this amounts to is that we cannot expect science to aid us here, neither with arguments *for* the indestructibility of the soul nor, and perhaps this is more noteworthy, with arguments *against* it.

Psychology might be somewhat more helpful, except for those of its branches which purport to be pure natural science. For example, the following statement, if it is so, might be considered an argument: "In the unconscious each of us is convinced of his own immortality." But the author of the sentence, Sigmund Freud,[20] deliberately disqualified it as an argument, even while insisting that it was based on empirical observation. And obviously it was a finding that could not remotely be compared with the result of an opinion poll.

To digress for a moment, opinion polling is virtually meaningless in the present case. A few years ago, in the course of a poll taken in six European countries, forty-seven out of one hundred Germans stated that they believed in immortality.[21] This fact obviously has not the slightest force as argument, if only because people questioned in such interviews express only what they *think* their opinion is. They may be speaking in good faith, but their real convictions about such subjects are usually of such a character that hasty questioning cannot get at them. Perhaps these real opinions will only become recognizable to the person questioned in some moment of existential shock.

The statement from Sigmund Freud is, I think, something quite different and must be taken far more seriously. One may very well wonder if all people, in the preconscious dimension of psychic life, should without exception be able to deceive themselves in regard to so fundamental an existential matter as "immortality".

Nevertheless, we are not yet examining an argument in the strict sense of the word—that is to say, a reason obtained by dealing cognitively with the subject under discussion itself.

Among the commonly cited reasons for the indestructibility of the soul there are, of course, dozens which do not satisfy this requirement. This does not mean that they are not well worth considering—as, for example, the Kantian idea that immortality can be "postulated" because without it there would be no basis for the absoluteness of moral obligation; or the reminder that men knew themselves to be in the right when they give up physical life for the sake of higher goals; or the universal human practice of religious burial of the dead—and so on.

But are there real arguments in the strict sense for the indestructibility of the soul, that is, reasons which follow from some insight into the reality of the soul itself? Arguments of exactly this sort have, at any rate, been repeatedly formulated for several thousand years. Every one of them, without exception, has to do one thing if their claims are not to collapse promptly. They have to do more than simply clarify a matter (by "simply" I mean: answering a question about a state of affairs with neutral, academic impartiality). Rather, these arguments must provide the ground to stand on and withstand the challenge of a seemingly irrefutable experience, the experience that in death all the vital manifestations of man cease, including those of his mind and spirit. The arguments, therefore, must show persuasively how the human soul is ultimately independent of the body, and that on the basis of its being, or more precisely, on the basis of that aspect of its being which is perceptible to us, it cannot be included in the obvious dissolution of the body. Quite a few of the "classical" arguments do in fact advance this thesis. Their cue words differ: "simplicity," "immateriality," "spirituality," "supratemporality," and so on.

Our list remains incomplete in any case, but we have not yet mentioned one argument which must be discussed in greater detail. Probably we all have an affinity, different for each of us, to one particular argument, so that the others do not mean too much to us. As far as I am concerned, the most persuasive argument derives from the "*capacity for truth*". It can be found in one form or another, incidentally, throughout the whole range of the tradition from Plato[22] and Augustine[23] to Thomas Aquinas. The angel and the human soul, says Thomas,[24] are imperishable, *incorruptibiles*, because they are by nature capable of grasping truth, *capaces veritatis*. Of course that is only the concluding sentence of a line of argumentation. No one can perceive the force of this argument unless he "sees" that cognition of truth, however it makes use of the physical senses, is essentially a process independent of all material concatenations. In fact, everyone recognizes this as so, whether or not he knows it; indeed, it is even recognized by those who explicitly and formally deny it. There are not many arguments of which this can be said. But is the assertion true? Let us see.

As soon as people really "speak", they are assuming their ability to recognize truth, if not that they have already recognized it. For speaking means to make reality recognizable and to communicate it. And truth is nothing but reality's being known.

Now of course not everything that comes from the mouth of *homo sapiens* is *eo ipso* human speech in that sense. If the stimulation of certain brain centres, as during an operation, sets in motion the speech mechanism, no one would call such "utterances" real speech, even if they should by chance yield a meaning. There is also a purely associative kind of thinking and speaking, blindly following impulses, which no doubt is likewise caused by psychic and physiological mechanisms. Logically sound "thinking the truth", on the other hand, might actually be defined as resistance to such freely offered associations. Above all, however, there is "ideological" thinking, that is to say, a kind of thinking determined more or less by material interests, not by the objective conditions, which is to say by truth.

The chief point is this: whenever someone charges that

such ideological thinking is "false consciousness", that is, whenever he rejects its claim to be "true", he is implying, probably without realizing it, that truth presupposes independence. Insofar as Marxism has made certain valid contributions, it is through its methodical principle of exposing the objective worthlessness of certain political or even "philosophical" theses *on the ground* that they are the outcome of material or economic conditions. This very type of demonstration makes it clear to us what we judge as true must be free from all non-mental causality. Even if someone were to declare that all human opinions without exception have come about as the consequence of mechanically operating necessity, as the result, say, of class and productive relationships, or as sublimations of the libido, he is still assuming that his own opinion is excepted.[25] He is absolutely compelled to do so. Why? Because otherwise he would be denying his own capacity to grasp reality; he would be denying the capacity of his soul for truth—and thus its indestructibility. Evidently no one is able to do that, with all its implications and consequences.

Reduced to its syllogistic form, the argument runs as follows: Because the human soul is capable of apprehending truth as such; because it is capable of this act which by its essence goes beyond every conceivable material concatenation and remains independent of it; because, thus understood, it is capable of an *operatio absoluta*—therefore it must also have an *esse absolutum*; it must possess a *being* independent of the body; it must be an entity that persists through the dissolution of the body and beyond death.[26]

What the nature of this continuance will be, and how the mode of existence of the "departed soul," the *anima separata*, may be conceived—concerning these matters there is no sub-stantiated human knowledge. And one can almost recognize the great minds by their abstaining from the claim to any such knowledge. We recognize them by their silence. Not only in Plato, but also in Thomas Aquinas[27] we find no speculation on what happens to man on the other side of death. Even the sacred books of Christendom, although they describe Eternal Life in a multitude of images, say scarcely a word about the mode of being of the dead—aside from their sometimes speaking of death as a "falling asleep".

This phrase, however, probably should be taken more literally than is usually done. Sleepers as well as others who are transported out of the body, are more receptive;[28] they enter a realm of existence in which a new non-temporal mode of duration reigns and in which our clocks and measure-ments of time no longer mean anything. The "interval", ex-tending from the moment of death to the Resurrection awaited by faith at the end of days, cannot possibly be of the same type of duration as the time between birth and death. Time, eon, eternity have become, from one moment to the next, and in an entirely new fashion, "simultaneous". This thought opens a wide field to meditation and the reflective imagination. But we are barred from going beyond more or less plausible conjectures—which does not mean that reason, seeking explanations, may not find such conjectures magnifi-cent and be enchanted by them.

One who is steeped in the empirical knowledge that the living person is a matter of the reciprocal influences of body and soul, and who regards death as the end of the real physical-spiritual man, stands mute and perplexed before the question of how a soul separated from the body is to be imagined as "existing" at all, let alone as "alive".

I believe that this perplexity cannot be dispelled by any amount of speculative thinking, whether it be philosophical or theological. But this very perplexity might possibly make the believed truth of the Resurrection audible in an entirely new way—not understandable but audible, or perhaps only somewhat more audible. Western theology has in fact said: because ultimate bliss also means the actual perfection of the blessed, and because the soul does not possess the perfection of its nature, not even the godlikeness it is capable of achieving, except in conjunction with the body[29]—therefore the indestructibility of the soul seems actually to require the coming Resurrection.[30]

This would signify, however, that the overcoming of death had not taken place yet, as indeed this same theology tells us. For there is also the Resurrection for the Judgment (John 5:29). Still less can that overcoming consist in the mere indestructibility of the soul. But since on the other hand what exists "by nature" (that is, "because of Creation") is always primary[31] and is the basis for every other divine gift that may be accorded to creatures, therefore, if the soul were not "by nature" indestructible there would simply be nothing and no one able to receive the immortality which truly conquers death, that gift for which the sacred tradition of mankind has devised countless names: Perfect Joy, Eternal Life, Great Banquet, Crown, Wreath, Peace, Light, Salvation—and so forth.

Thus we have now at last touched, and perhaps somewhat overstepped, the boundary which is set for the philosophical inquirer. Really to reach this boundary—therein lies, I think, the true meaning and distinctive opportunity of philosophy. The great philosophers have always seen in philosophy a challenge to penetrate beyond philosophizing. If this challenge presents itself to us more sharply than usual in the present case, this only indicates once more that death is a philosophical subject in a special sense, as we said at the outset.

To those remarks with which we began, let us add, by way of close, the stern reminder of Sören Kierkegaard: "Honour to learning, and honour to one who can treat the learned question of immortality in a learned way. But the question of immortality *is* no learned question. It is a question of the inner existence, a question which the individual must confront by looking into his own soul."

Notes

The authors of the three epigraphs are Jean-Paul Sartre, Samuel Beckett and Pope John XXIII. The original French and Italian texts are as follows:

Il est absurde que nous soyons nés, il est absurde que nous mourions, J.-P. Sartre, *L'Etre et le Néant* (Paris, ¹⁸1949), p. 631; *Being and Nothingness,* translated by Hazel E. Barnes (New York: Philosophical Library, 1956), p. 577.

Ogni giorno è buono per nascere; ogni giorno è buono per morire. Discorsi, Messaggi, Colloqui del Santo Padre Giovanni XXIII, vol. V (Rome, 1964), p. 310.

I

1. Hermann Volk, *Das christliche Verständnis des Todes* (Münster, 1957), p. 8.
2. Augustine, *Confessiones,* 4, 4, 9.
3. Paul Ludwig Landsberg, *Die Erfahrung des Todes* (Lucerne, 1937), pp. 53 f.
4. Arthur Schopenhauer, *Sämtliche Werke* (Leipzig: Insel-Verlag, n.d.), vol. 2, p. 1240.
5. Cicero, *Tusculanae Disputationes,* I, 75.
6. Dominicus Gundissalinus, *De divisione philosophiae,* edited by Ludwig Baur (Münster, 1903), p. 7.
7. Cassiodorus, *De artibus et disciplinis liberalibus,* cap. 3, Migne, *Patrologia Latina,* vol. 70, 1167.
8. *Horum [philosophorum] te mori nemo coget, omnes docebunt.* Seneca, *De brevitate vitae,* 15, 1.
9. Epictetus, *Discourses,* II, 1; 36.
10. Michel de Montaigne, *The Complete Works of Montaigne,* newly translated by Donald M. Frame (Stanford University Press, 1957), p. 62.

11. Plato, *Phaedo*, 107 c 4.

12. Augustine, *Soliloquia* II, 1.

13. Max Scheler speaks of the "type of modern man" who "gives little thought to life after death chiefly because he at bottom denies the core and essence of death"; he alone has found no symbol for death "because it is not there for experiencing". Max Scheler, *Tod und Fortleben, Schriften aus dem Nachlass*, vol. 1 (Berlin, 1933), pp. 8, 26. The English anthropologist and sociologist Geoffrey Gorer declares ("The Pornography of Death", in *Encounter*, October 1955; reprinted in *Death, Grief and Mourning. A Study of Contemporary Society* [Garden City: Anchor Books, 1967], p. 197): "It seems symptomatic that the contemporary sect of Christian Science should deny the fact of physical death even to the extent (so it is said) of refusing to allow the word to be printed in the *Christian Science Monitor*." Even the (American) undertakers try, by special "language regulations", to leave the fact of dying unmentioned as far as possible. "So have the funeral men managed to delete the word death and all its associations from their vocabulary." Jessica Mitford, *The American Way of Death* (New York, 1963), p. 77.

14. Hans Urs von Balthasar, "Der Tod im heutigen Denken", in *Anima*, No. 11 (1956), p. 293.

15. Achim Mechler, "Der Tod als Thema der neueren medizinischen Literatur", in *Jahrbuch für Psychologie und Psychotherapie*, 3 (1955), p. 371.

16. Martin Heidegger, *Being and Time*, translated by John McQuarrie and Edward Robinson (Edinburgh and New York, 1962), pp. 284, 282.

17. Karl Jaspers, *Psychologie der Weltanschauungen* (Berlin, 1919), p. 231.

18. Adolf Faller, "Biologisches von Sterben und Tod", in *Anima*, 11 (1956), p. 265.

19. John Henry Newman, *Grammar of Assent* (London, 1892), p. 36 f.

20. Scheler, *Tod und Fortleben*, p. 9.

21. Augustine, *Commentary on the Psalms*, 38, 19.

22. Augustine, *Sermones* 97, 3; 3.

23. Montaigne, *Complete Works*, p. 61.

24. E.g., *Phaedo* 64 a.

25. Edward Young, *Works* (London, 1774), vol. III, p. 17.

26. Martin Heidegger, *Being and Time*, p. 297.

27. Gabriel Marcel, *The Mystery of Being*, vol. II: *Faith and Reality* (Chicago, 1960), p. 171.

28. P. L. Landsberg, *Die Erfahrung des Todes*, p. 32. Gabriel Marcel also says something similar: "In a world in which the arid influence of technique seems to prepare the radical disappearance of intersubjective relations, death would no longer be a mystery, it would come as a raw fact like the dislocation of some piece of mechanism." *The Mystery of Being*, p. 169.

29. Thomas Aquinas, *Commentary on the Sentences* 3 d. 35, 1, 21. The dictum comes from Richard of St Victor.

II

1. Quoted in Viktor-Emil von Gebsattel, "Aspekte des Todes", in *Synopsis. Studien aus Medizin und Naturwissenschaften*, Heft 3 (Hamburg, 1949), p. 62.

2. *Ibid.*

3. Quoted in Eugen Korschelt, *Lebensdauer, Altern und Tod* (Jena, ³1924), p. 405.

4. *Ibid.*

5. Viktor-Emil von Gebsattel, "Aspekte des Todes," p. 62.

6. Cf., for example, Acts 13:36.

7. Sören Kierkegaard, *Religiöse Reden*, translated by Theodor Haecker (Leipzig, 1936), p. 159 ff.

8. "It is common, especially in pious language, to have a dying man say he is passing from time into eternity." Thus Immanuel Kant begins his treatise written late in life (1794), "Das Ende aller Dinge", in *Gesammelte Schriften* (Prussian Academy of Sciences edition), vol. 8, p. 327.

9. *Sit humus cineri non onerosa tuo*, Ovid, *Amores*, III, 9; 68.

10. I Cor. 15: 26, 55.

11. Euripides, *Alcestis*, first act, first scene. Cf. also Homer, *Iliad* 16, 672 f.; likewise Hesiod, *Theogony*, 212; 756 ff.

12. Georg Simmel, *Rembrandt* (Leipzig, 1917), pp. 91, 94.

13. Epicurus, *On the Overcoming of Fear*. Ernst Bloch, too, has recently repeated the old sophism. *Das Prinzip Hoffnung* (Frankfurt a.M., 1969), p. 1391.

14. Of March 19, 1827.

15. Johann Wolfgang von Goethe, *Tag-und-Jahreshefte 1807. Autobiographische Schriften* (Insel edition), vol. 3, p. 536.

16. Hans Urs von Balthasar, "Der Tod im heutigen Denken," p. 296.

III

1. *Phaedo*, 64 c 4; similarly, *Gorgias*, 524 b 2.

2. Cf. Adolf Faller, *Biologisches von Sterben und Tod*, p. 266.

3. Thomas Aquinas, *Compendium Theologiae*, 1, 230; no. 483.

4. Thus Karl Rahner, *Zur Theologie des Todes* (Freiburg i. Br., 1958), p. 18. Still one might cite Ecc. 12:7: "And the dust returns to the earth as it was, and the spirit returns to God who gave it."

5. Karl Rahner, *Zur Theologie des Todes*, p. 18.

6. *Ibid.*, p. 19.

7. Plato, *Alcibiades*, 129 e 11; 130 c 5.

8. Etienne Gilson, *History of Christian Philosophy in the Middle Ages* (New York, 1955), p. 361 f.

9. Thomas Aquinas, *Summa theologica*, I, 75, 4.

10. Karl Jaspers, *Three Essays: Leonardo, Descartes, Max Weber.* Translated by Ralph Manheim (London and New York, 1964), p. 153.

11. Cf. Jacques Maritain, *Three Reformers* (London and New York, 1929). The chapter on Descartes is entitled "Descartes or The Incarnation of the Angel", p. 51.

12. Cap. 16.

13. *The Meditations of Marcus Aurelius* (Chicago, 1956), 4, 41.

14. Arthur Schopenhauer, *Sämtliche Werke*, vol. 5, p. 293.

15. *Ibid.*, vol. 2, p. 1250.

16. Thus in the international periodical *Novum Testamentum*, No. 2 (Leiden, 1957), p. 158, in a review of Oscar Cullmann's essay, "Unsterblichkeit der Seele und Auferstehung von den Toten" (*Theologische Zeitschrift* No. 12, 1956; Festgabe für Karl Barth).

17. Hermann Volk, *Das christliche Verständnis des Todes*, p. 26.

18. Cf. Cullmann, "Unsterblichkeit der Seele und Auferstehung von den Toten", p. 128.

19. I Cor. 15:53 f.; I Tim. 6:16.

20. *Summa theologica*, I, 97, 1; I, 97, 4; I, 76, 5 ad 1.

21. *Summa contra Gentes*, 4, 82.

22. J. G. Fichte, *Die Anweisung zum seligen Leben, oder auch die Religionslehre*. 6. Vorlesung. *Werke*, ed. Fritz Medicus (Leipzig, 1911 ff.), vol. 5, p. 200.

23. Plato, *Apology*, 34 e 2.

24. *Ibid.*, 34 d 4.

25. Plato, *Phaedo*, 111 b 7.

26. Thomas Aquinas, *Summa theologica*, I, 75, 4.

27. . . . *ex ratione humanae naturae, ad quam pertinet verum corpus habere*. *Summa theologica*, III, 5, 1.

28. *Quaest, disp. de spiritualibus creaturis*, 2 ad 5.

29. *De unitate intellectus*, 1, 6: *Anima unitur corpori non sicut nauta navi sed sicut forma.*

30. *Quaest. disp. de potentia Dei* 5, 10 ad 5: *Anima corpori unita plus assimilatur Deo quam a corpore separata quia perfectius habet suam naturam.*

31. Although the Council of Vienne (1311-12) had declared the proposition of the *anima forma corporis* an obligatory dogma of the Church.

32. Oscar Cullmann, "Unsterblichkeit der Seele und Auferstehung von den Toten", p. 138.

33. Thomas Aquinas, *Summa theologica*, I, 50, 5.

34. *Phaedo*, 115 c 4.

35. 1, 15; No. 108.

36. Norbert Luyten in *Unsterblichkeit* (Basel, 1957), p. 17.

37. C. S. Lewis, *Miracles. A Preliminary Study* (London, 1947), p. 154.

38. *L'homme étant un composé d'âme et de corps, l'âme séparée n'est pas un homme. Elle reste un être humain, évidemment, et même . . . un être qui a acquis son ultime perfection naturelle. C'est en ce sens qu'à cet endroit et à quelques autres, on l'appelle homme.* Emile Mersch, *La théologie du Corps Mystique* (Bruges, ⁴1954), vol. 1,

p. 152. "As to what degree of aliveness is possessed by the soul still existing after death because of its indestructible spiritual reality, no certain statement is part of the creed; the still existing soul is not the man." Hermann Volk, *Handbuch theologischer Grundbegriffe*, vol. 2 (Munich, 1963), p. 672.

39. *Anima separata est pars rationalis naturae, scilicet humanae, et non tota natura rationalis humana, et ideo non est persona. Quaest. disp. de potentia Dei*, 9, 2 ad 14. Cf. also *Summa theologica*, I, 29, 1 ad 5; I, 75, 4 ad 2.

40. Helmut Thielcke, *Tod und Leben. Studien zur christlichen Anthropologie* (Tübingen, ²1946), p. 195.

41. Hans Urs von Balthasar, "Der Tod im heutigen Denken", p. 294.

IV

1. Plato, *Symposium*, 189 d 6.

2. To Karoline von Wolzogen. *Schillers Leben* (Tübingen, 1830), p. 268 ff.

3. Jean-Paul Sartre, *Existentialism and Humanism*, translated by Philip Maret (London, ⁴1960), p. 28.

4. Jean-Paul Sartre, *Being and Nothingness* (London and New York, 1956), p. 533.

5. Arthur Schopenhauer, *Sämtliche Werke*, vol. 2, p. 1288.

6. *Ibid.*, vol. 2, p. 1295.

7. Max Scheler, *Tod und Fortleben*, p. 19.

8. Epictetus, *Dicourses*, IV, 7; 15.

9. Hermann Volk, *Das christliche Verständnis des Todes*, p. 14.

10. Romano Guardini, *Die letzten Dinge* (Würzburg, 1952), p. 14.

11. Cullmann, "Unsterblichkeit der Seele und Auferstehung", p. 137; cf. also Note 13.

12. *Maximen und Reflexionen*, ed. Günther Müller (Kröners Taschenausgabe), No. 505.

13. To Riemer; June 1807.

14. *Gespräche mit Eckermann*; February 15, 1830.

15. Thomas Aquinas, *Compendium Theologiae* 1, 227; No. 477.

16. *Ibid.*, No. 475.

17. *Quaest. disp. de veritate*, 26, 6 ad 8.

18. Quoted in Joachim Wach, *Das Problem des Todes in der Philosophie unserer Zeit* (Tübingen, 1934), p. 27.

19. Friedrich Hölderlin, Letter to Neuffer of May 8, 1795.

20. Friedrich Nietzsche, *Gesammelte Werke*. Musarion-Ausgabe (Munich, 1922 ff.), vol. 13, p. 120.

21. *Ibid.*, vol. 19, pp. 185, 347.

22. *Ibid.*, vol. 16, p. 225.

23. *Ibid.*, vol. 19, p. 174.

24. *Ibid.*, vol. 10, p. 74.

25. Walter Kaufmann, *Philosophic Classics. Thales to St Thomas* (Englewood Cliffs, N.J.: Prentice-Hall, Inc., 1961), p. 9.

26. Plato, *Symposium*, 193 a 2.

27. Seneca, *De ira*, 1, 16.

28. Karl Peters, "Strafe", in *Staatslexikon*, vol. 7 (Freiburg i. Br., 1966), col. 730.

29. C. S. Lewis, *The Problem of Pain* (London, 1940), p. 82.

30. Thomas Aquinas, *Summa contra Gentes*, 4, 90: *Poena proportionaliter debet culpae respondere.*

31. Thomas Aquinas, *Quaest. disp. de malo* 1, 4; *Summa theologica* I, II, 46, 6 ad 2.

32. Dionysus Areopagita, *De divinis nominibus* 4; § 22; 213. Cf. the commentary of Thomas Aquinas 4, 18; No. 527.

33. Thomas Aquinas, *Summa theologica*, II, II, 19, 1.

34. Augustine, *Confessiones* 10, 28, 39. Thomas Aquinas, *Summa theologica*, II, II, 34, 2 ad 3.

35. Augustine, *De libero arbitrio* 1; Fulgentius, *De fide ad Petrum* (formerly thought to be a work of Augustine's), cap. 21. Thomas Aquinas, *Quaest. disp. de malo*, 1, 4; *Summa theologica*, I, 48, 5; *Commentary on the Sentences*, 3 d. 34, 2, 3, 1.

36. Romano Guardini, *Die letzten Dinge*, pp. 13 f.

37. Sigmund Freud, "Zeitgemässes über Krieg und Tod": *Gesammelte Werke* (London, 1946 ff.), vol. 10, p. 341.

38. Karl Jaspers, *Psychologie der Weltanschauungen*, p. 231.

39. Arthur Schopenhauer, *Sämtliche Werke*, vol. 2, p. 1270.

40. Jacques Maritain, *Von Bergson zu Thomas* (Cambridge, Mass., 1945), p. 146.

41. Thus Alfred Bertholet in *Religion in Geschichte und Gegenwart*, 2nd ed., vol. 5, col. 1190.

42. Karl Rahner, *Zur Theologie des Todes*, p. 49.

43. *Ibid.*, p. 50.

44. *Ibid.*, p. 49.

45. *Summa contra Gentes* 4, 50 (1).

46. Arthur Schopenhauer, *Sämtliche Werke*, vol. 2, p. 1295.

47. Thus one might say in analogy to Augustine's sentence: We see things because they are; but they are because God sees them. *Confessiones*, 13, 38; *De Trinitate*, 6, 10.

48. II, II, 164, 1 ad 1.

49. *Quaest. disp. de malo*, 5, 5 ad 17.

50. *Commentary on the Sentences*, 3 d. 16, 1, 1.

51. Alfred North Whitehead, *Adventures of Ideas* (New York, 1956), pp. 290 f.

52. Karl Rahner, *Zur Theologie des Todes*, p. 45. Similarly, Hermann Volk: "According to Scripture, the destructive power of sin finds its clearest expression in the deadly violence of death." *Handbuch theologischer Grundbegriffe*, vol. 2, p. 672.

53. Cf. Thomas Aquinas, *Summa theologica*, I, 97, 1.

54. *Ibid.*, I, 76, 5 ad 1.

55. Karl Rahner, *Zur Theologie des Todes*, p. 33.

56. *Quaest. disp. de malo*, 5, 5. Cf. also *Summa theologica*, II, II, 164, 1 ad 1; *Compendium Theologiae*, 1, 152.

57. *Si ad naturam corporis respiciatur, mors naturalis est.* Thomas Aquinas, *Compendium Theologiae*, 1, 152.

58. *Mors non est naturalis homini ex parte suae formae.* Thomas Aquinas, *Summa theologica*, II, II, 164, 1 ad 1.

59. *Anima amisit virtutem qua posset suum corpus continere immune a corruptione.* Thomas Aquinas, *Quaest. disp. de malo*, 4, 3 ad 4.

60. *Aptitudo quaedam naturalis ad eam* [=*immortalitatem*] *convenit homini secundum animam. Ibid.*, 5, 5.

61. *Christus autem mortuus est non necessitate, sed potestate et propria voluntate.* Thomas Aquinas, *Compendium Theologiae*, 1, 230; No. 483.

62. *Commentary on the Sentences*, 3 d. 16, 1, 1 ad 5.

63. Cf. Ernst Bloch who calls "the certainty of class consciousness" "a *novum* against death" and "a remedy for death". *Das Prinzip Hoffnung*, pp. 1380, 1383.

64. Teilhard de Chardin calls death "the necessary lever in the mechanism and upsurge of life." *The Phenomenon of Man*, translated by Bernard Wall (London and New York, 1959), p. 310. But on the whole, of course, Teilhard de Chardin cannot be termed a representative of "ideological evolutionism". Cf. Josef Pieper, *Hope and History*, (London and New York, 1969), pp. 55 ff.

65. Martin Heidegger, *Being and Time*, pp. 435 ff., 311.

66. Thomas Aquinas, *Summa theologica*, II, II, 164, 1 ad 5.

67. *Per mortem naturalem non purgatur aliquis de peccato actuali, sed per mortem illatam bene potest purgari*. Thomas Aquinas, *Commentary on the Sentences*, 4 d. 20, 1, 3 ad 3. Cf. also 4 d. 21, 1, 3, 2 ad 3.

68. Simone Weil, *Gravity and Grace*, translated by Arthur Wills (New York, 1952), p. 121.

69. Karl Rahner, *Zur Theologie des Todes*, p. 45.

70. Plato, *Gorgias*, 478.

71. *Grundlinien der Philosophie des Rechts*. Ed. Johann Hoffmeister (Hamburg, 1955), p. 96.

72. *Sämtliche Werke*, Jubiläumsausgabe. Ed. Hermann Glockner (Stuttgart, 1958), vol. 16, p. 25. Cf. also vol. 3, p. 47.

73. *Ibid.*, vol. 1, p. 485.

74. C. S. Lewis, *Miracles*, p. 157.

V

1. To J. D. Falk, January 25, 1813.

2. Cf. Karl Rahner who distinguishes between the "natural" and the "personal" aspect of death. *Zur Theologie des Todes*, p. 15.

3. Pascal, *Pensées*, No. 172 (L. Brunschvicg).

4. Gabriel Marcel, *Être et Avoir* (Paris, 1935), p. 117.

5. *Being and Nothingness*, p. 538.

6. *Das Prinzip Hoffnung*, p. 285.

7. Ernst Bloch, *Philosophische Grundfragen,* I (Frankfurt a.M., 1961), pp. 15 f.

8. *Hoc enim est hominibus mors, quod angelis casus*; what the moment of testing is for angels, death is for man. This sentence from John of Damascus (*De fide orthodoxa*, II 4) is frequently quoted by Thomas Aquinas, though the wording may differ somewhat; e.g. in *Commentary on the Sentences*, 2 d. 7, 1, 2; 4 d. 1, 3; in the *Quaest. disp. de veritate*, 24, 10, sed contra 4; in the *Summa theologica*, I, 64, 2.

9. Thomas Aquinas, *Quaest. quodlibetales*, 9, 8 ad 2.

10. Aside from Karl Rahner chiefly: Ladislaus Boros, *The Moment of Truth: Mysterium Mortis* (London and New York, 1965). Palémon Glorieux, "In hora Mortis", in *Mélanges de Science Religieuse*, 6 (1949). Palémon Glorieux, "Endurcissement final et grâces dernières", in *Nouvelle Revue Théologique*, 59 (1932). Lucien Roure, "Le décisif passage", in *Études*, 1928. Roger Troisfontaines, *Ich sterbe nicht* (Freiburg i. Br.-Basel-Vienna, 1964). Émile Mersch, *La théologie du Corps Mystique* (Paris, 1944).

11. Roger Troisfontaines, *Ich sterbe nicht*, pp. 140 ff.

12. Karl Rahner, *Zur Theologie des Todes*, p. 85.

13. *Ibid.*, p. 58.

14. Roger Troisfontaines, *Ich sterbe nicht*, pp. 141, 167.

15. Ladislaus Boros, *op. cit.*, p. 9.

16. Roger Troisfontaines, *Über den Tod* (Paderborn, 1954), p. 59.

17. Friedrich Nietzsche, "Die Unschuld des Werdens". *Der Nachlass*, ed. A. Bäumler (Leipzig, 1931), vol. 1, p. 363.

18. Palémon Glorieux, "Endurcissement final", p. 887.

19. Jean-Paul Sartre, *Being and Nothingness*, p. 533.

20. *Ibid.*, p. 539.

21. Cf. *Du hast mich heimgesucht bei Nacht. Abschiedsbriefe und Aufzeichnungen des Widerstandes* 1933-1945 (Munich, 1954), p. 223.

22. Martin Heidegger, *Being and Time*, p. 288.

VI

1. Karl Rahner, *Zur Theologie des Todes*, p. 77.

2. Roger Troisfontaines, *Ich sterbe nicht*, p. 138.

3. Sören Kierkegaard, *Christentum und Christenheit*, ed. and tr. Eva Schlechta (Munich, 1957), p. 243.

4. "But in the hospitals it has become the custom to deflect the

dying man from his death. By the dubious deception that he is still far from death, the dying man is alienated from his death. Obviously this stratagem is meant just as much for the comforter himself." Achim Mechler, *Der Tod als Thema der neueren medizinischen Literatur*, p. 382.

5. In *Synopsis. Studien aus Medizin und Naturwissenschaft*, Heft 3 (Hamburg, 1949).

6. Plato, *Gorgias*, 522 e 1.

7. *Bewusstes Sterben*, p. 23.

8. Ernst Jünger, *Jahre der Okkupation* (Stuttgart, 1958), p. 179 ff.

9. *Being and Nothingness*, p. 630.

10. *Ibid.*, p. 539.

11. Ladislaus Boros, "Pilgerstand", in *Lexikon für Theologie und Kirche*, 2nd ed., vol. 8, col. 507 f.

12. Palémon Glorieux, "In hora Mortis", p. 213.

13. Thomas Aquinas, *Summa theologica*, I, II, 53, 3 ad 3.

14. Cf. Lucien Roure, "Le décisif passage", p. 405 ff.

15. Cf. Josef Pieper, *Happiness and Contemplation* (London, 1959; New York, 1958), p. 87.

16. Viktor Emil von Gebsattel, *Aspekte des Todes*, p. 86.

17. Cf. for example Henri Bon, *La Mort et ses problèmes* (Paris, 1947), p. 25 ff.

18. Karl Rahner, *Zur Theologie des Todes*, p. 86.

19. Michel de Montaigne, *Complete Works*, p. 60.

20. Georges Bernanos, *Dialogues des Carmélites* (Paris, n.d.), p. 54.

21. Jean Hild, "Der Tod als christliches Mysterium", in *Anima*, 11 (1956), p. 213.

22. Cf. on this Hermann Volk, *Das christliche Verständnis des Todes*, p. 83.

23. "Only one single time, namely, dying, can he give back his life, which death is robbing him of, in union with the dying Lord his Creator and the Father of our Lord Jesus Christ, give it back in such a way that he loses it." *Ibid.*, p. 83.

VII

1. *Being and Nothingness*, p. 538.

2. Helmut Thielicke, *Tod und Leben*, p. 182.

3. Gerardus van der Leeuw, *Phänomenologie der Religion* (Tübingen, 1933), p. 294.

4. *Novum Testamentum*, No. 2, p. 138.

5. Cf. Hans Urs von Balthasar, "Der Tod im heutigen Denken," p. 295 (". . . So that the resurrection of the body almost seems little more than an 'accessory fact' which could just as well be omitted").

6. Helmut Thielicke, *Tod und Leben*, p. 100.

7. Carl Stange, *Die Unsterblichkeit der Seele* (Gütersloh, 1925), p. 134.

8. *Ibid.*, p. 12.

9. Norbert Luyten in *Unsterblichkeit*, p. 11. Thomas Aquinas likewise says: "Innumerable (*infinitae*) are the testimonies of Holy Scripture which witness the immortality of the soul." *Summa contra Gentes*, 2, 79.

10. Hans Urs von Balthasar, *Der Tod im heutigen Denken*, p. 299.

11. Hermann Hettner, *Geschichte der deutschen Literatur im 18. Jahrhundert*, ed. G. Witkowski (Leipzig, 1928), vol. 2, p. 141.

12. Paragraph 56; it contains only this one sentence.

13. Carl Stange, *Die Unsterblichkeit der Seele*, p. 105.

14. *Ibid.*, p. 99.

15. Nietzsche speaks of the "great lie of personal immortality". *Gesammelte Werke*, vol. 17, p. 22.

16. Immanuel Kant, *Kritik der praktischen Vernunft*, ed. Karl Vorländer (Leipzig, [7]1920), p. 156.

17. Hermann Samuel Reimarus, *Abhandlungen von den vornehmsten Wahrheiten der natürlichen Religion* (Tübingen, [5]1782), chap. 10, Sect. 5, p. 796.

18. P. 61.

19. *Einige Vorlesungen über die Bestimmung des Gelehrten*, 3. Vorlesung. *Werke*, vol. 1, p. 250 f.

20. Simone Weil, *Gravity and Grace*, p. 84.

21. Thus it is hard to understand what Karl Beth in *Religion in Geschichte und Gegenwart* (2nd ed., vol. 5, col. 1398) seems to be saying, that *for this historical reason* the concept of immortality has been dismissed from the dogmatic discussion of contemporary Protestant theology as not pertinent.

22. "The teachings of the great Socrates, of the greater Plato,

cannot be reconciled with those of the New Testament." Oscar Cullmann, "Unsterblichkeit der Seele und Auferstehung von den Toten,"
p. 156. "Immortality is an idea of Greek philosophy, and this idea has
nothing to do with the Resurrection of the Bible." *Novum Testamentum*, No. 2, p. 158.

23. Moses Mendelssohn, *Phädon oder über die Unsterblichkeit der
Seele* (Reutlingen, ⁴1789), p. vi f.

23a. As the author of this book, who transformed Platonic dialogues into television plays. Cf. Josef Pieper, *Kümmert euch nicht um
Sokrates* (Berlin, 1966).

24. Cf. Hermann Hettner, *Geschichte der deutschen Literatur im
18. Jahrhundert*, vol. 2, p. 138.

25. Plato, *Phaedo*, 107 c 4.

26. *Ibid.*, 113 e 5.

27. In *Unsterblichkeit*, p. 49.

28. Moses Mendelssohn, *Phädon*, p. 182.

29. Plato, *Phaedo*, 111 b 7 f.

30. Oscar Cullmann, "Unsterblichkeit der Seele und Auferstehung
von den Toten," p. 155.

31. Plato, *Phaedrus*, 246 c.

32. Ervin Rohde, *Psyche. Seelenkult und Unsterblichkeitsglaube
der Griechen*, 9-10th ed. (Tübingen, 1925), vol. 2, p. 2.

VIII

1. *Handbuch theologischer Grundbegriffe*, vol. 2, p. 672.

2. In *Unsterblichkeit*, p. 38. But cf. also Karl Jaspers, *Philosophie*
(Berlin-Göttingen-Heidelberg, ²1948), pp. 753 ff.

3. *Commentary on the Metaphysics*, 10, 12; No. 2145.

4. V, 31; *scholion*.

5. *Gespräche mit Eckermann*; May 2, 1824.

6. Arthur Schopenhauer, *Sämtliche Werke*, vol. 2, p. 1271.

7. *Ibid.*, p. 1261.

8. *Commentary on the Sentences*, 1 d. 8, 3, 2.

9. *Quaest. disp. de potentia Dei*, 5, 9 ad 1; similarly *ibid.*, 5, 4 and
Summa theologica, I, 104, 4.

10. *Quaest. disp. de potentia Dei*, 5, 4 ad 10.

11. *Sicut solus Deus potest creare, ita solus potest creaturas in nihilum redigere.* Thomas Aquinas, *Summa theologica*, III, 13, 2.

12. Thomas Aquinas, *Qaest. disp. de potentia Dei*, 5, 4 ad 6; similarly, *Commentary on the Sentences*, 4 d. 46, 1, 3 ad 6; 2, 2, 1 ad 4.

13. Thomas Aquinas, *Quaest. quodlibetales*, 4, 4.

14. In *Unsterblichkeit*, p. 46.

15. Thomas Aquinas says that non-spiritual creatures *secundum substantiam* (*Quaest. disp. de potentia Dei* 5, 4) or *in suis causis* (*ibid.*, 5, 9 ad 1) are imperishable.

16. Paul Althaus, *Die letzten Dinge* (Gütersloh, [4]1933), p. 90 f.

17. Gottfried Wilhelm Leibniz, *Neue Abhandlungen über den menschlichen Verstand* (Darmstadt, 1959), pp. lvi f.

18. In *Unsterblichkeit*, p. 29.

19. *Ibid.*, p. 21.

20. Sigmund Freud, *Gesammelte Werke*, vol. 10, p. 341.

21. Karl Friedrichs, *Lebensdauer, Altern und Tod* (Frankfurt a.M., 1959), p. 199.

22. *Phaedo*, 79.

23. *De Trinitate*, 13, 8.

24. *Summa theologica*, I, 61, 2 ad 3.

25. Cf. on this, C. S. Lewis, *Miracles*, p. 30.

26. Thomas Aquinas, *Commentary on the Sentences*, 2 d. 19, 1, 1.

27. Thomas does indeed discuss questions such as the mode of cognition of the soul after death (e.g. *Quaest. disp. de veritate*, 19, 1). But he proceeds explicitly from the truth of the *creed* (*Sicut firmiter secundum fidem catholicam sustinemus . . . ita sustinere necesse est . . .*).

28. Cf. Thomas Aquinas, *Quaest. quodlibetales*, 3, 21; *Summa contra Gentes*, 2, 81.

29. Thomas Aquinas, *Quaest. disp. de potentia Dei*, 5, 10 ad 5.

30. Thomas Aquinas, *Summa contra Gentes*, 4, 79.

31. Thomas Aquinas, *Summa theologica*, I, II, 17, 9 ad 2; *Quaest. disp. de veritate* 16, 2 ad 5.

32. Sören Kierkegaard, *Samlede Vaerker*, vol. VII (Copenhagen, 1902), pp. 143 f.